BRITISH STEAM LIVES!

BRITISH STEAM LIVES!

COLIN GARRATT

AB		MM	
MA		MN	
MB		MO	
MC	12\05	MR	
MD		MT	
ME		MW	
MG			
MH			

First published in Great Britain in 1984 by
Blandford Press

This edition published 2005 by Bounty Books,
a division of Octopus Publishing Group Ltd
2–4 Heron Quays, London E14 4JP

Copyright © Octopus Publishing Group Ltd 1979, 2005

ISBN 0 7537 1064 1
ISBN13 9780753710647

A CIP catalogue record for this book is available from the British Library

Printed and bound in China

Contents

Author's Note

The author wishes to acknowledge his use of Canon Cameras and Agfachrome Film, along with the support he has received from Electrosonic (Audio Visual) Ltd. and *Steam Railway Magazine*.

Introduction

I feel a great sense of pride in being one of the last individuals in Britain to earn a living from the steam locomotive. I feel proud to be associated with the magnificent locomotive building traditions pioneered by Britain over one and a half centuries both at home and abroad.

Few people would doubt that the steam railway brought immense benefits to mankind. It was a manageable and civilised technology and if only progress could have been halted when the railway age was at its height and the rabid degeneration into road transportation averted our world would be a happier and healthier place today.

The great railway builders are now little more than legendary names in industrial history and the generations of proud and skilled craftsmen have almost disappeared. But tributes to their memory and testimonials to their achievements must be passed on – either by picture, word or artefact – in order that new generations of Britons can be told one of the most exciting of all industrial tales.

My commitment to find and document what is left is now a lifetime's endeavour. But in the enormity of my self-imposed task I draw strength from that great vitality of spirit which was once – and is tragically no longer – the essential characteristic of Britain's railway industry.

Colin Garratt
Newton Harcourt
February 1984

1 The End of an Era

Britain was the mother country of railways and the steam locomotive was possibly Britain's greatest technological gift to the world. From its inception in 1804 on an ironworks line in South Wales, the steam locomotive had changed the face of Britain by the middle of the nineteenth century, following 20 years of railway mania in which the building of lines proceeded at a phenomenal pace. In 1845 alone, 623 new lines were proposed, and by 1848 Britain could boast of having 5,000 miles of main-line railway.

The advent of the steam railway allowed the industrial revolution to 'take wings' as for the first time a properly coordinated transport system was available, and although the canals were the industrial triumph of the eighteenth century, they constituted a poor method of transport for heavy materials, and thus retarded the inherent dynamism of British industry.

Although Britain's lead in pioneering the railway age was dramatically manifested at home, her influence spread across the world. The export of locomotives began during the 1830s, and many countries received their first steam locomotives from Britain. A large percentage of the locomotives and rolling stock built by Britain were exported, and although certain other 'industrialising' countries such as France, Germany and America soon began their own building traditions, it fell to Great Britain to finance, build and provide equipment for many of the world's railways.

That Britain should do this for her vast empire was inevitable, but there were few countries where Britain's interests were not paramount in railway affairs. There were, of course, many other aspects of industrial achievement in which Britain was globally influential; Britain was, as the saying goes, 'the workshop of the world', but in that workshop the speciality was railways – and these provided a cornerstone for Britain's industrial and commercial interests.

The great foundries which grew up to produce the locomotives have now become legendary names in industrial history: Robert Stephenson of Newcastle-upon-Tyne founded in 1829 the first locomotive works in the world; the Vulcan Foundry of Newton-le-Willows, Lancashire; Beyer Peacock of Manchester; Sharp Stewart, Neilson and Dubs, all of Glasgow, to mention a few important examples.

These foundries are quite distinct from those which were owned by Britain's private railway companies. As the home network grew, an inevitable amalgam of smaller lines took place to form such famous names as Midland Railway, London and North Western Railway, Great Western Railway, and literally dozens of others. Most of these companies preferred to design and build their own locomotives, and it was the erection of these workshops which gave rise to the one time 'railway towns' like Swindon, Crewe, Doncaster and Derby.

The private builders, although often supplying the home railway companies with locomotives (usually to the railway companies' designs), concentrated largely upon the export market along with the needs of the innumerable small industrial establishments such as collieries, mines, docks, power stations and ironworks. The workshops of the railway companies did not intrude on the private builders' domain. Attempts were made in this direction, but the practice was very quickly nipped in the bud by powerful representations made by a consortium of private builders.

Nevertheless, there was an inevitable interaction between these two areas of locomotive building, and throughout the nineteenth century most of Britain's locomotive exports mirrored the type of engine which ran in the mother country. Where the gauges were either narrower or wider than the standard British 4 ft. $8\frac{1}{2}$ in. (such as one metre, or 5 ft. 6 in.) the engines were simply scaled in proportion, and the 'shape of the day' remained fundamentally unaltered.

Britain's supremacy as locomotive builder to the world remained largely unchallenged throughout the nineteenth century. Around 1900, however, serious competition was encountered for the first time, especially from America and Germany. America had, by this time, fully equipped her home railways and was keen to develop a thriving export market to keep the huge foundries – with their mass production capacity – operational.

Quite apart from the commercial threat, America's engines posed a challenge to conventional British design which, though excellent and the product of skilled craftsmen, did on occasions have deficiencies which were not apparent at home but caused problems in the rough and tumble of the world's railways.

American engines were invariably tough two-cylinder types with bar frames, wide fireboxes, excellent bearing surfaces, and many labour saving devices; what these engines lacked in craftsmanship, they gained in price. In contrast, most British locomotives up to the turn of the century had small fireboxes set between the frames and the inevitable restriction in size could cause problems with inferior coal. The traditional British plate frames were often cited as another weakness, especially when the engine ran on tracks which were of poor quality. Hot bearings were another source of trouble for certain engines under adverse conditions.

One immediate effect of America's aggressive export drive was the amalgamation in 1903 of the three big Glasgow builders Sharp Stewart, Neilson and Dubs to form the North British Locomotive Company. Increasing foreign competition inevitably heralded a shift towards a more 'international' design of locomotive, born in the light of world experience. Britain retained a leading role right until the end of steam, her later export packages including many exciting designs unknown on the home networks.

Some famous foundries disappeared during the depression of the 1930s, but the decline of steam traction on a global scale from the 1950s onwards led to the demise of almost all Britain's locomotive builders. After a vigorous history of steam building they were not well suited to supply a world which demanded mass-produced diesels from new high investment companies in Canada, the U.S.A. and the advanced countries of Europe.

The final exports of British steam locomotives in the early 1960s were undertaken without ceremony. More public attention was paid to the remarkable renaissance which occurred in 1971, when Hunslet of Leeds built an 0-4-2ST for a sugar factory in Java. This historic little engine laggardly followed the tens of thousands of magnificent machines which, having been built by proud craftsmen, rolled onto the decks of ships bound for all corners of the earth. One consoling factor remains in that many of these fine engines survive in active service today, and a few are over 100 years old.

The demise of Britain's export industry coincided not only with the demise of steam building at home, but even worse, the demise of the railway itself. Following the British Transport Commission's decision in 1954 to phase out steam traction came the widespread running down of the railway network in favour of a transport system based upon roads.

That vested interests by oil companies, motor vehicle manufacturers and contracting firms played a significant part in this process can hardly be doubted, but the vast majority of Britons played directly into their hands by making a demi-god of the family car. The road lobby had all it needed to press ahead with motorways, and the scene was set for the traditionally humble lorry to turn into the juggernaut.

The Beeching years gave a further sop to the railway's decline and as a large part of the network was shut down, the remainder was inevitably weakened. Manufacturing complexes which had traditionally been built with rail access were sited well away, making them dependent upon roads.

It is a strange paradox that in 1950, when Britain had some 25,000 steam locomotives, she also had a comprehensive network of railways which went virtually everywhere and served most communities. This comprehensive, disciplined and safe transport system ran on our indigenous reserves of coal.

That this should be rejected in favour of a motive power which burns imported fuel is one thing, but to switch to the hideous inefficiencies of a transport policy based upon 13 million cars and upwards of a million lorries is quite another! The annual carnage on Britain's roads of 6,000 dead and 24,000 injured is in itself more than sufficient to render the road system totally unacceptable. If one adds to this the attendant squandering of oil reserves as if there were no tomorrow, combined with the environmental destruction and anti-social effects of the road system − not least in large cities − one can only yearn for the return of a comprehensive railway network to provide an efficient and civilised transport system.

My underlying suggestion is that we should not mourn the passing of steam simply because it was aesthetically exciting, but we should also mourn it for what it represented as a national transport system, run with a masterly pride in the job. That pride of service which was once so characteristic of the railway, has today degenerated into personal gratification as manifested by that symbol of decadent squander − the family car.

Although the mother country has turned its back on railways, they remain in our blood; they are part of our national heritage and thus of our identity, and it is fitting that Britain should lead the world in railway preservation.

The railway preservation movement in Britain seeks to provide a permanent glimpse of past glories, and miracles have been achieved, but they must not only concern themselves with preserving the past. The movement needs to mobilise Britain's millions of railway enthusiasts into a powerful fighting lobby, to retain what is left of the national railway and expand it.

Such militancy by all railway lovers, in a national crusade, would be of inestimable service to Britain and would be the most fitting salute to those pioneers who so righteously laid our railway system down. Even as I write these words, news has been given of proposals for another round of line closures, including that masterpiece the Settle and Carlisle.

One final point needs to be made: there is an increasing concern that railway preservation (in the museum sense) has been restricted almost exclusively to Britain's indigenous networks, with no heed being paid to Britain's role as railway builder to the world – the other half of the story! Hopefully this situation is about to change, and when it does, a new and dynamic understanding of Britain's railway history will be made.

Overleaf: The end of a Stanier Black 5 at Cohen's Breakers Yard, Kettering. No less than 855 of these superb engines once ran the length and breadth of Britain. They were highly capable and performed excellently on a wide variety of duties and were greatly respected by their crews. As economic all rounders, the Black 5s were retired prematurely by a British Railways' management hell bent on creating a 'new image' for the railway. Tragically that 'new image' involved shutting down half the network and turning to imported fuel to operate the part that was left.

Left: The death of the steam age in Britain coincided with the partial death of the railway itself. In the 'new image' era, the significance of Britain's railway system was allowed to shrink to a level which was nothing short of a national scandal. The atmosphere of those final years during the 1960s – when a heritage was abandoned – is conjured up in this scene at Patricroft depicting Stanier 8Fs on the left whilst on the right is a British Railway's Standard 5 4–6–0. This engine – a mere 13 years old – was waiting to be towed away for scrapping!

Overleaf: The remains of another Black 5 at Cohen's Yard, Kettering. In the front left foreground can be seen the tubes which have been cut from the engine's boiler.

The leading wheels of a Stanier 8F disappear beneath a blaze of acetylene at Cohen's Breakers Yard. Notice the axle boxes clinging to the axle and the way in which the torch has cut through the wheel in the right foreground.

2 Preservation of the Heritage

Railway preservation in Britain constitutes a miracle; over 1,500 locomotives have been preserved and some 60 running lines secured. Some of these museum lines have reached splendid maturity, such as the $14\frac{1}{2}$-mile long Severn Valley Railway which runs between Bridgenorth and Foley Part, near Kidderminster. Others are in the embryo stage, with perhaps only a mile or two of track, although extensions are envisaged in most cases.

Thirty years ago, the steam locomotive had an indefinite future in Britain. Few people felt the need for preservation and even lifelong railway observers like Cecil J. Allen were confidently writing in the late 1950s that steam in Britain would last into the twenty-first century. How dramatically and unpredictably times change and how wrong the most expert of experts can be!

Commensurate with the demise of Britain's steam railways came the 'official list' stating the items which were to be preserved. Not only was this list extremely limited in scope but it had been set out by a governmental bureaucracy. Railway enthusiasts had no part in the process; they were seen – both by themselves and by the railway administration – as being quite distinct from railway operations and never should the two meet.

When the historic campaign to save the Welsh Talyllyn Railway was launched by enthusiasts in 1951, the general response was almost vitriolic – enthusiasts operating and running a railway? Ridiculous and impossible! As we know, the Talyllyn pioneers won the day and laid the foundations for everything that has been achieved since.

Today, 30 years later, little credit for the magnificence of railway preservation in Britain can go to the State for if matters had been left to the government controlled institutions the results would have been meagre. Not only did the aspirations of the 'official list' bear false witness to the heritage in question but the scheduled exhibits were only for stuffing and mounting, not for keeping in running order.

Following the success of the Talyllyn project, preservation involving enthusiasts went from strength to strength and as both steam traction and railway alike were decimated during the 1960s, there was much to achieve in a desperately short space of time. British enthusiasts wished to see a far wider range of exhibits under preservation and they wanted them running in their full glory. Subsequently, under the guidance of the Association of Railway Preservation Societies (A.R.P.S.) the movement as a whole has not only achieved miracles but has brought the pleasure of railways to the public at large in addition to those too young to have known a steam railway.

The entrepreneurial brilliance of the British railway preservation movement is marred, however, by its sole concern for artefacts which actually operated in Britain. Virtually no interest has been shown in Britain's global railway heritage. The National Railway Museum should have provided the lead years ago but has consistently failed to do so and thus put in jeopardy this magnificent aspect of the country's history. Fortunately, this deficiency should now be made good but, once again, the necessary spirit and imagination is being provided by private individuals.

I have spent the last 15 years professionally documenting the world's surviving steam railways, yet I never fail to be amazed by the sheer monumentality of our forefather's achievements – not just in locomotive building – but in the whole range of manufacturing and technical skills required to run a railway.

As railway enthusiasts, we are not only blessed with an insight into one of the most exciting periods of industrial history, but more significantly we are entrusted with that history. It is behoven upon each and every one of us to recognise this and to take some responsibility for the generations to come. The continual proposals for the opening of new lines in Britain along with the scheme to rescue the remaining engines in Barry – though entirely laudable in principle – will demand vast resources, which for the time being, should be put to more enlightened use.

Every day of every week of every year, classic British locomotives, rolling stock and archives, are being destroyed all over the world by countries which have little or no awareness of an industrial past. Future generations will not forgive us for permitting this destruction; they will not share the petty prejudices of today's enthusiasts, many of whom only wish to preserve the locomotives they remember from childhood. Generations to come will make no such distinction and a once famous type of engine which ran on the Southern for example, will be no more interesting than a Clyde-built one exported to the Empire.

I know from meeting a wide cross section of people during my nationwide shows that considerable concern exists within the country about the direction railway preservation in Britain is taking. Many questions are raised and fears expressed that unless something is done about our overseas heritage, an incalculable opportunity will have been lost. It was with this in mind that I read an article called 'Preservation Priorities' which appeared in the Friends of the National Railway Museum's newsletter No. 14 (February 1981) in which G. C. Dickinson called for an end to the Barry humbug and entreated the Museum to take the lead in a new initiative. He wrote: 'if this generation really does love railways, it must bequeath to its successors a sound legacy which does full justice to the global empire which Britain built.'

The great Valhalla envisaged by Dickinson was for a separate working museum to reflect the role Britain has played in the development of world railways. Unfortunately, the response he received was lacking in enthusiasm to say the least. A negative disclaimer was appended by the editor, whilst the museum itself failed to respond. This did not deter Dickinson from renewing his challenge to bureaucratic complacency when one year later he wrote in the same newsletter and in the same context: 'Your heritage lies rotting in a foreign field. Awake England and Scotland too, ere it is too late.'

Further glimmers of a new dawn came when Ron Fitzgerald, Keeper of the Leeds Industrial Museum wrote to me with a view to repatriating the last Kitson Meyer 0–6–6–0 from the Atacama Desert of Chile. However, the rumpus I had caused in Chile about the uniqueness of this engine possibly helped to get it preserved, as shortly after Ron contacted me, the engine was declared a Chilean National Monument.

For me personally, the lack of vision shown by the entire preservation establishment for anything beyond Dover, has been particularly frustrating as I have worked on countless threatened railways on which items should be preserved – either in their country of operation, or set by for possible return to Britain. My position has been an invidious one, as to this day my researches remain entirely self-funded and I have never had – or been offered – wherewithal to make the necessary representations to foreign governments. The best I can do is make a fuss locally in the hope that someone will listen. Sometimes this is successful and in late 1982 I received a letter from the Azores Ministry of Culture informing me that the two 7 ft. 0$\frac{1}{4}$ in. broad gauge engines that I unearthed on Sao Miguel island have now been taken to a local museum after 10 years rotting in a scrapyard.

The case of the last high speed British Pacific – which survived in Bengal until 1981 – was infinitely more desperate. I was

Above: The building of the Benguela Railway (Caminho de Ferro de Benguela (C.F.B.)) showing the finished road bed near Cubal in 1910 and the terrain of the Corrotiva Mountains. (B.O.R.H.S. – C.F.B. Archives)

Below: A celebration in the Angolan bush near Silva Port *c.*1925 with a 6th class 4–6–0 built by North British of Glasgow in 1906. The engine is heading a contractor's train of vans and bogie opens. (B.O.R.H.S. – C.F.B. Archives)

actually at Burdwan depot when the telegram came from Eastern Railway H.Q. to despatch XC class No. 22224 for breaking. With the help of depot foreman Bajpai and the divisional manager, I had the engine hidden away pending my own preservation attempt. This was in outright defiance of H.Q.'s instructions, but the engine ended so great a tradition in British locomotive history (William Stanier and E. S. Cox both having worked on XCs half a century previously) that something had to be done.

I mention these two examples because despite *Steam Railway Magazine* reporting both stories in full – the broad gaugers occupied four pages in issue 22 and the XCs five pages in issue 16 – not a glimmer of interest was shown by the preservation establishment. Not so much as a 'phone call or a postcard came from the people whose official responsibility is to preserve our railway heritage. In contrast, I received many communications from individuals asking how these priceless relics could be saved.

Dozens of other instances could be quoted, but allow me to mention one more which concerns the beautifully styled standard gauge 4–4–4Ts lying derelict in Uruguay. These Lancashire-built engines are almost identical to the Wirral Railway's 4–4–4Ts of 1896 which were the first examples of this short-lived but highly elegant phase of mid-period suburban engines. If such a locomotive were discovered derelict in Britain, there would be an avid scramble to have it preserved, but because it is called 'foreign', the present establishment is unable to relate to it or care about it. How can such relics be denigrated as 'foreign' when they were designed and built in the heart of England for railways which were financed, constructed, owned and operated by the British?

Quite apart from being unique, these period 4–4–4Ts represent one of the missing evolutionary links amongst the ranks of British preserved steam. If one considers that relics such as these are being officially spurned in favour of preserving the thirteenth Bulleid Pacific, the fifteenth Black 5 or the sixtieth Hunslet Austerity, then it becomes obvious that our present policies are clearly and emphatically wrong.

Then, one evening in May 1982 another glimmer of hope emerged when John Scott Morgan, chairman of the newly formed British Overseas Railway Historical Society (B.O.R.H.S.), telephoned me – quite out of the blue – with an invitation to become one of the society's trustees. I knew little of his organisation at the time, but his obvious concern for responsible and enlightened preservation was backed up by several recent successes, not least the return to Britain – in full working order – of the Pakistan Railway's SPS class inside-cylinder 4–4–0 No. 3157 (Vulcan Foundry, 1922). The SPS was the second Lancashire-built engine

B.O.R.H.S. had secured as they played a significant role in the acquisition of a Manchester-built EM2 electric locomotive from Holland.

John and I agreed to meet and he told me with great enthusiasm how the society had made a last minute rescue of the complete Benguela Railway archives. These priceless records show in graphic detail how this amazing railway was built and they contain documents, glass negatives, maps, tickets, publicity material and guide books, along with civil and mechanical engineer's drawings on all aspects of a railway pioneering project at the turn of the century in Africa. The comprehensiveness and clarity of these archives literally represents a time capsule for future historians on this masterpiece of British enterprise.

The society's objective is to create a large working museum which will do full justice to the role Britain played in the building of the world's railways. Apart from such obvious assets as locomotives and rolling stock, the society places considerable emphasis upon the kind of archives already mentioned and efforts will be made to coordinate these within a properly constructed museum to show how the pioneering railways developed agriculture and industry and thus heralded important changes in the social order.

It was obvious that the society's aims were quite different from the traditional approach to railway preservation and it was felt that the Science Museum would be the most appropriate body to reflect our aspirations. Accordingly, a meeting was arranged for John and myself along with the society's president – broadcaster Anthony Burton – to meet Tony Hall-Patch, the Keeper of Railways at the Science Museum. Our concern was put over with candour and we presented a proposal that the society – in the form of a charitable trust – should assist in the identification of appropriate items, negotiate terms with their overseas owners, arrange transport back to Britain and, most important of all, raise the necessary funds. In return, we requested that the Science Museum provide a specific site.

A list of the society's trustees was formally handed over to the Museum: Anthony Burton, author, broadcaster and president; John Scott Morgan, railway historian, founding member and chairman; Michael Bailey, railway historian and officer of the Manchester Ship Canal; Peter Phillip, solicitor; and myself. It was agreed that three further trustees would be appointed – a financial advisor, a mechanical engineer and a representative of the museum authority.

Tony Hall-Patch responded enthusiastically to our proposals as the Science Museum had prepared a tentative list of overseas items for possible preservation. He felt that a further meeting was

Above: 6th class 4–6–0 No. 361 at Pretoria with a train of ex-Netherlands South African Railway Company four wheel stock *c.* 1901 (B.O.R.H.S. Archives)

Below: Unloading maize from a standard 20-ton bogie open wagon at Lobito Harbour on the Benguela Railway. Over one million of these wagons remain at work on the railways of Africa and they are the most common railway vehicle in regular use. (B.O.R.H.S. – C.F.B. Archives)

necessary to explore the project in greater depth with the head of the Science Museum, Dame Margaret Weston.

At this meeting John Scott Morgan, Anthony Burton and myself met Dame Margaret along with Tony Hall-Patch and Brian Lacey, Chief of the Transport Department. The urgent need to begin an overseas collection was accepted in principle by the museum. It was also agreed unanimously that the society would not indulge in the indiscriminate collection of items simply because they were available and that one of the main criteria in respect of locomotives and rolling stock would be to show significant differences from their counterparts built for the home market.

We proposed that the overseas museum should be located on a site sufficiently large enough to incorporate a stretch of running line with simulated colonial characteristics. This could be based on the Benguela Railway to complement the archives already in the society's possession. The Benguela has expressed a willingness to cooperate in the return of a mountain-type Garratt with Lentz poppet valves along with a wooden-bodied day coach built by Metro Cammell in 1929.

The availability of a suitable site was discussed in some detail and two possibilities emerged. One was to utilise available land in York and the other was to develop the overseas collection as part of the Science Museum's Roughton complex. Roughton lies five miles from Swindon and is a former R.A.F. aerodrome. The site occupies several square miles and is intended to house the considerable overspill of transport items currently in the Science Museum's collection.

It was decided that the society's trustees should visit both sites along with representatives of the Science Museum prior to holding a further meeting. In addition to a specific overseas collection, the society would support regional museums with the acquisition of items pertinent to local industries – the very situation which Ron Fitzgerald in Leeds had been seeking.

As far as locomotives are concerned, the overseas museum could embrace such items as Mallets, Kitson Meyers, Garratts, Twelve Wheelers (4–8–0), Mikados (2–8–2), Mountains (4–8–2), Confederations (4–8–4) and Berkshires (2–8–4) – types which hardly appeared in Britain but were featured in export shipments. Obviously scope would exist for the purely homespun product and high on my personal list would be the Indian XC Pacific and a Uruguayan 4–4–4T. The B50 class 2–4–0 from Java is also high in the popularity stakes and negotiations to acquire one have already begun. Some of these engines remain at work, having been exported from Sharp Stewart's works on Great Bridgewater Street, Manchester over a century ago!

The last greyhound of British steam, Indian Railway's XC class No. 22224 on the day that she was withdrawn from service at Burdwan depot in Bengal. This picture

represents the culmination of 10 days spent with this engine owing to its unique place in the history of British steam traction. The team I worked with are shown from left to right: S. K. Sarkar (driver), Sachin Roy (firing instructor), S. N. Bajpai (depot foreman), Author, Margaret Grzyb, Santosh Chaudhuri (depot chargeman), S. A. Ansari (loco cleaner). On the footplate is T. P. Ghosh (fireman).

No XCs are scheduled to be preserved in India and no one in Britain has expressed serious interest in repatriating one. In 25 years time such short sightedness will be seen as inexcusable.

Left: Awake England – and Scotland too – ere it is too late, your heritage lies rotting in a foreign field. Eloquent truth to this testimony is provided by this scene of classic British inside-cylinder 0–6–0s being broken up at Sultanpur.

Overleaf: Superb British locomotives for the railways of the world. For half a century this engine hauled 1,500-ton coal trains over the hill regions of Bengal. Today, the wheel has come full circle for this mighty XE class 2–8–2, so magnificently forged on the Clyde by William Beardmore in 1930 for the East Indian Railway.

One of Britain's greatest locomotive builders was Sharp Stewart who began building in Manchester before moving to a larger site in Springburn, Glasgow in 1887. This plate which belongs to a saddle tank in Brazil shows the year in which Sharp Stewart merged with Dubs and Neilson Reid to form the North British Locomotive Company.

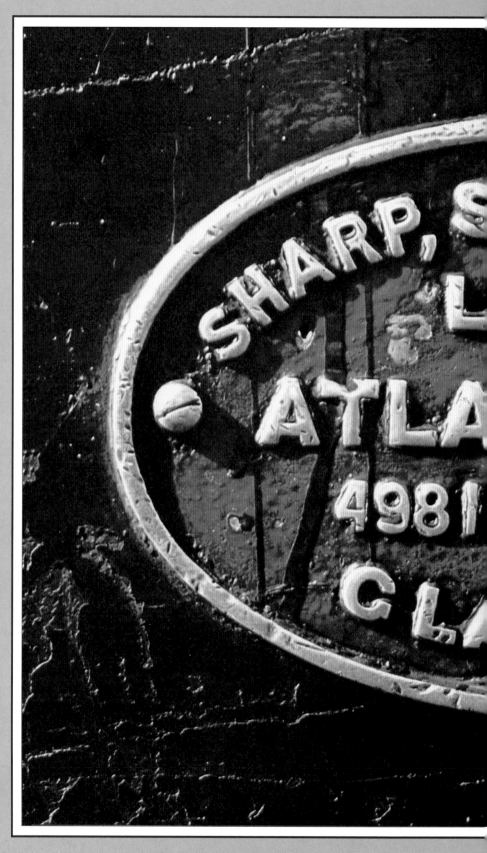

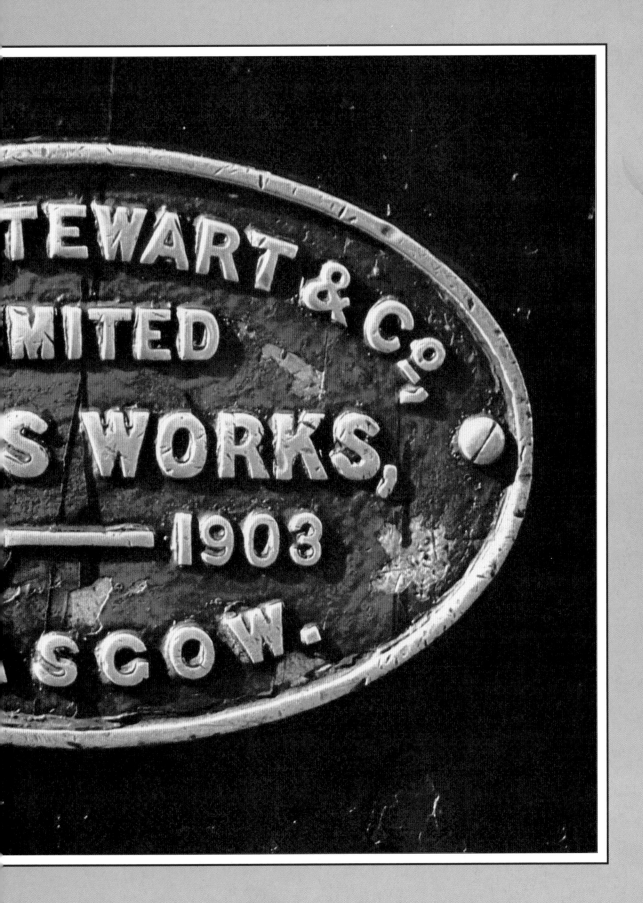

3 Surviving Early Forms

The steam locomotive's ability to survive to a great age is one of its most alluring features. Few people, whether rail buffs or not, fail to be attracted by a wheezy old veteran which soldiers on, against all odds, long beyond the average human life span. At a time when steam traction is being decimated all over the world, it is heartening to know that some of the very earliest forms of locomotive can still be found at work, and that a few of them are over a century old.

The ability of these old timers to survive reminds us of the pride and skill which went into their manufacture. They were built by craftsmen long since dead, and whose descendants have almost certainly passed from railway service. Such engines also remind us of an age not blighted by inbuilt obsolescence; an age when man's creations were built to last.

Without attempting to deride the dignity of old locomotives, it must be remembered that over the years many will have seen an extensive renewal of parts, if not an actual rebuilding. A few are analogous with 'grandpa's axe', which over the years received various new handles and cutting heads. There is, of course, no absolute criteria since some engines, in appearance at least, remain almost unaltered, and it is absorbing to examine a 90-year-old engine to try to ascertain the degree of mechanical and visual change which has taken place over the years. There are many cases where frames, wheels, boiler shells and tenders are all original, as with the locomotives illustrated in this chapter.

One of the principal early forms of locomotive was the 0—4—0. When I was a small boy I did not think that such engines ever ran in the real world; I thought they were a figment of Hornby's imagination – the kind of engine that only whizzed around those clockwork trainsets of childhood. Undoubtedly the most famous 0—4—0 of all time was George Stephenson's *Locomotion*, which was built in Darlington in 1825 for hauling coals between Stockton and Darlington.

My childhood imaginings about the 0–4–0 were not far removed from the truth as, despite being a fundamental early form of locomotive, it quickly disappeared when freight and passenger engines began to polarise into their respective progressions. The 0–4–0 as a mineral hauler clearly did not provide sufficient adhesion and rapidly evolved into the 0–6–0. As a passenger engine, the 0–4–0 was quickly superseded either by single wheelers or 2–4–0s, both of which provided better stability for running at speed. The best known group of 0–4–0s were those of Edward Bury, which saw extensive use on the London and Birmingham Railway and later on the Furness, for whom building continued until the 1860s. In evolutionary terms, the 0–4–0 was an early form of mixed traffic engine which flowered before the concept of a mixed traffic engine proper was generally needed.

Although the 0–4–0 disappeared from Britain many years ago, two fascinating examples survive in India. Named *Tweed* and *Mersey* respectively, they hailed from Sharp Stewart's works on Great Bridgewater Street, Manchester in 1873, 14 years before the company moved their premises to the Glasgow suburb of Springburn. These 110-year-old, metre-gauge veterans worked on the Tirhut Railway and in 1874 provided important famine relief by connecting Tirhut with Patna 100 miles away. Following use as mixed-traffic engines on main-line work, both engines gravitated into service at sugar factories. Sharp Stewart's engines have a reputation for longevity, but the remarkable survival of these veterans has been aided by their only working during the milling season, the off season being given over to care and maintenance.

Seeing these two engines at work is like being back in a distant age, and the aura of vintage is quite startling. Both are remarkably well preserved although *Tweed* is better cared for. Neither factory has any intention of putting these engines out of service.

Other isolated examples of 0–4–0s exist, most notably the Indonesian State Railway's B52 class. Built during the early twentieth century, these superheated examples are a latterday flowering of the type and were almost certainly the last ones built for main-line use.

If the 0–4–0 represented an early form of mixed traffic, it quickly evolved into the 0–4–2, the most famous example being *Lion*, built in 1838 for the Liverpool and Manchester Railway. This veteran recently came to national fame by taking part in the Rainhill Cavalcade of 1980. The 0–4–2 achieved some prominence at home and featured in early export packages. Its final years of development coincided with the need for a mixed traffic engine proper, and some notable examples were produced in Stroudley's D2s of 1876 for the London Brighton and South Coast Railway; these engines paved the way for Adam's Jubilees introduced in 1887 for the London and South Western Railway.

The only British 0–4–2 to survive is Stroudley's *Gladstone*, miraculously saved by the Stephenson Locomotive Society during the 1930s. This was the first time a group of enthusiasts had become involved in railway preservation and, although an isolated incident at the time, it did create a precedent for the system we have today.

The only standard-gauge 0–4–2s left today lie derelict in Java where several have languished since World War 2. These engines were built by Beyer Peacock and the oldest dates back to 1883. They are relics of the former Dutch NIS, a company involved in the piecemeal construction of Java's southern main line from Jakarta to Surabaya, which operated a standard-gauge section between Jogjakarta and Surakarta as opposed to the remainder which was 3 ft 6 in. gauge.

During World War 2, the Japanese invaded Java and looted all the standard-gauge track for trans-shipment to Manchuria. In the long term this gave Java a unified gauge, but left the 0–4–2s in isolation.

Much discussion has taken place about the possibility of returning one to Britain, and since my visit to Java in 1974, I have received many letters on the subject. Though an exciting prospect, one can only assume that, having lain in their tropical enclave for almost 40 years, the engines are in too poor a state ever to run again.

The only other British 0–4–2 known to exist is of Scottish origin. In contrast, this engine is in full running order, and works on the metre-gauge section of a sugar factory in Bihar. She was formerly an E class engine, believed to have been built in 1878 by Dubs for the Indian State Railway, but in common with *Tweed* and *Mersey* has since gravitated to the sugar fields. Again, in common with her 0–4–0 relatives, she works the factory connection with the metre-gauge main line of Indian Railways – the plantations proper being built to a gauge of 2 ft. 6 in.

As far as the purely passenger designs are concerned, the mainstream of evolution began with either the Single or 2–4–0. The first true passenger engine was Stephenson's *Rocket* of 1829, an 0–2–2 Single, whose large wheel was deemed necessary for running at speed. *Rocket* actually ran at 39 m.p.h., an unprecedented speed for 1829! As speeds increased, greater stability was called for, and thus the 2–2–2 Single was developed, which was then followed by the 4–2–2 which first appeared during the 1840s.

The Singles were extremely fleet-footed, and as a concept were to remain as a significant express passenger type throughout the remainder of the nineteenth century; the final ones for service in Britain were not actually completed until 1901. Many Singles were exported, the last being a batch of extremely handsome 4–2–2s from Kerr Stuart's works in Stoke-on-Trent in 1910, for China's Shanghai and Nanking Railway. These gorgeous engines were decked in Chinese Imperial yellow, and closely resembled the Midland Railway's Spinners, upon which the design was clearly based.

Throughout my researches and world expeditions, it has long been my ambition to discover a Single, but after 15 years of trying I have not even managed to locate a derelict one. Some years ago, a member of the Newcomen Society claimed that some examples of the Shanghai and Nanking still existed in China, but this now seems extremely doubtful. Nevertheless, so beautiful and significant was the Single in British locomotive history, that I still cherish my dream, but fear that time may have run out and that the Single is now extinct.

The first 2–4–0s appeared during the 1830s and were adopted by many home railways over successive decades, in addition to being prolifically exported. The 2–4–0 possessed a better pulling and starting ability than the Single, and the most famous example was the London and North Western Railway's 'Jumbo' No. 790 *Hardwicke* which, as part of the competition between east and west coast routes during the railway races to Scotland in 1895, ran the 141 miles from Crewe to Carlisle at an average speed of 67.2 m.p.h.

The 2–4–0 finally disappeared from Britain in 1949, when the last of Johnson's Midland Railway engines were broken up. Despite the large numbers exported over the years, the only ones to be found today are in Java, where an amazing enclave of 3 ft. 6 in. gauge 2–4–0s operate the decrepit branch line from Madiun to Slahung.

In common with the 0–4–0s mentioned earlier, these Javan veterans came from Sharp Stewart's Great Bridgewater Street works in Manchester in 1880, having been built for Java's State Railway. These engines are all the more interesting in being directly traceable back to the heyday of the 2–4–0 in Britain, before it gave way to the 4–4–0.

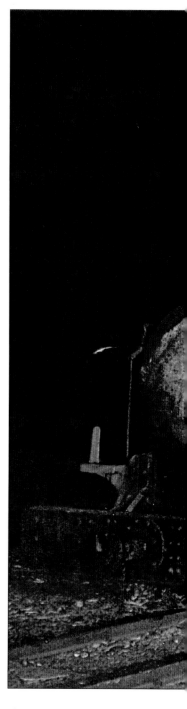

Above: The world's oldest working steam survivor caught in fiery mood during the early hours of the morning. She is a rare metre-gauge 0–4–0 tender engine named *Mersey* –

after the English river – and was exported from Sharp Stewart's works on Great Bridgewater Street, Manchester in 1873. She remains hard at work on an Indian sugar plantation and is one of the last surviving examples of this early form of locomotive.

Overleaf: Mersey has a sister called *Tweed* which also gravitated to service on sugar plantations following withdrawal from main-line service.

Left: The historic *Mersey* impatiently blows off from her safety valves as she awaits the signal to run onto the main-line network with a loaded train from the factory. Notice the nameplate – doubtless the original as manufactured by Sharp Stewart 111 years ago!

Above: The last 2–4–0 passenger hauling tender engines on earth can be found on Java. Classified B50, they are original Sharp Stewart (Manchester) engines and this example, No. B5014, was exported from their Great Bridgewater Street works in 1885. The oldest example of this class on Java dates back to 1880 – a time when the 2–4–0 was still being constructed as one of Britain's principal forms of express passenger locomotives.

Overleaf: The 0–4–2 is another early wheel arrangement now on the verge of extinction. Possibly the only example of this type still at work is No. 3, a metre-gauge veteran which survives in sugar-plantation service in India.

No. 3 is an enigma as she carries two different works plates; one proclaims her to be Vulcan Foundary No. 817 of 1877, and the other Neilson No. 2156 of 1876! Further confusion arises in that 22 identical engines are said to have been built by Dubs for the Indian State Railways in 1878.

At least two identical engines were subsequently shipped from India to Uganda but as far as is known No. 3 is the only surviving example of her type.

sleepy lineside villages provides unforgettable memories. The evenings were sheer magic, for my accommodation overlooked the line and I used to sit outside in the balmy night air with a cigar and a glass of whisky watching the incomparable delights of this Edwardian steam railway – a situation which put me as close to Paradise as I might reasonably expect to get.

Beyer Peacock exported several batches of Moguls before the turn of the century, including examples for Australia and Brazil. The Brazilian batch consisted of 15 wood-burning engines for the metre-gauge Leopoldina Railway in 1899, and when I was exploring the sugar plantations of Campos State in 1978 I was delighted to discover one example still active, having been pensioned off from main-line duty many years previously.

The discovery of this engine was doubly exciting as I had no knowledge of its existence, and in fact I very nearly missed it as she was far out in the fields when I visited the factory. Language difficulties prevented me from getting a description of the engine, and it was touch and go whether I stayed to investigate. Directions given by the yard manager seemed clear enough but I became hopelessly lost; one road degenerated into a quagmire, whilst the other ended in the middle of a field of cane.

I returned to the factory and begged for a guide, but even then it took us an hour to locate the engine, by which time the sun was beginning to set. But the effort was well worthwhile as she was undoubtedly the last survivor of the class.

Uruguay has been a major user of British Moguls since the early years of the century, although unfortunately only a handful remain active today. Uruguayan railways were British financed and constructed, and most of the locomotives came from Beyer Peacock's Gorton works. It has been suggested that the Manchester connection with the Fray Bentos Meat Company had something to do with that city providing so many of Uruguay's engines. Indeed, on my visit in 1979, Paysandu depot had over 30 locomotives – including derelicts; almost all were Beyer Peacock's and none was more recent than 1929.

In Uruguay, as in Paraguay, the Mogul is employed in its original American mixed-traffic role by working medium-sized trains over routes on which traffic is moderate – chiefly the fertile cattle rearing plains around Fray Bentos.

In view of Britain's close association in the development of Uruguayan Railways, the British Overseas Railway Historical Society is examining the possibility of repatriating certain exhibits. The first choice, as far as locomotives are concerned, would be one of the priceless 4–4–4T suburbans exported from Lancashire in 1915, but a Beyer Peacock Mogul would rate as a worthy second.

A mixed freight heads away from San Salvador bound for the Paraguayan capital Asuncion. The engine is a typical North British Mogul which was built in the Glasgow suburb of Springburn in 1910. These 'maids of all work' have monopolised services over Paraguay's standard-gauge main line for three-quarters of a century.

No. 59 is another of the 14 Moguls supplied by North British to Paraguay in 1910.
Notice the brass bell on the boiler top and the tender piled high with freshly cut logs.

Right: The classic Uruguayan Mogul.
Here is No. 88, the first example of 28 N
class Edwardian Moguls built by Beyer
Peacock between 1906 and 1910. In
common with their Paraguayan
counterparts, these all-purpose 2–6–0s
have performed superbly for over
three-quarters of a century.

56

5 The Incredible Bagnalls of the Assam Coalfield

In our story of British locomotives around the world, I felt it would be interesting to highlight just one set of engines in a particularly fascinating part of the world. The engines are the Staffordshire-built Bagnalls which survive on the Assam Coalfield in the north-eastern corner of India, some 25 miles from the Burmese border, and about 100 from that with Communist China.

The town of Stafford became known all over the world for the superb locomotives which came from Bagnall's Castle Engine works. The company began building steam locomotives in 1876, and throughout its long history concentrated chiefly upon industrial designs. Some main-liners were built but invariably for gauges less than standard.

The pride and skill adopted by successive generations of Bagnall employees is well known to railway historians, and the company is remarkable for the wide variety of its products. When Bagnall completed their last steam locomotive in 1956, the total for the 80-year period came to 1,667. It is refreshing to know that although Bagnall is now but one of many great names in British railway history, many of the company's engines remain active throughout the world.

In common with most industrial builders, Bagnalls did have some standard designs and the Assam engines are comprised of part of a family of saddle tanks built with innumerable detail variations over many years.

The engines were supplied to the Assam Railways and Trading Company, a British concern set up to develop the wealth of Upper Assam. As a prelude to these operations, British pioneers had sailed from Calcutta in Scottish-built paddle steamers and plied their way up through the waterways of what is now Bangladesh, and on into the mighty Brahmaputra River to sail due eastwards towards China. They entered the dense, inhospitable and leech-ridden jungles of Assam to develop thriving industries, tea gardens, timber and coal. It was inevitable that British saddle

Left: Sally takes a breather between duties on the Tipong network. *Sally* was built by Bagnalls of Stafford in 1930 and epitomises the narrow-gauge industrial which saw service throughout the world.

59

tanks should follow their enterprise. Nigh on a century later these emblems of the British Raj soldier on as if they will never die.

The Assam Railway and Trading Company was founded in 1881 and the first Bagnall arrived on the coalfield in 1894. In the same year an identical engine was delivered to the Jokai Tea Company. Named *Pekoe Tip*, this engine worked on the newly developed tea plantations which were to become universally acclaimed for the full-bodied flavour of Assam tea – in marked contrast to the fragrance of that from neighbouring Darjeeling.

In all, the coalfield received 15 locomotives built between 1894 and 1931, and 10 survive in active service. The first four were 0–4–2s with $5\frac{1}{2}$ in.-diameter cylinders, which in the following two engines delivered in 1899 had been increased to 6 in. From 1904 onwards the wheel arrangement was changed to 0–4–0 with a cylinder diameter of 7 in.

The engines work from several hillside mines, in conditions which no diesel could tolerate. The track is rough and uneven, and during the rainy season it often degenerates into a quagmire. At present, the coalfield yields half a million tons per year, principally for use in Assam. It is this localised usage which has enabled the steam stud to survive. The coalfield is extremely remote and the high transport costs to India at large have ensured that operations remain modest in output and thinking.

By far the biggest problem for the regional workshops in Margherita is maintaining the locomotive boilers, and already many of the Bagnalls are running on greatly reduced pressures, some on only 80 p.s.i. compared with their original 150 p.s.i., accordingly restricting the haulage capacity. However, by a combination of dogged persistence and the steam locomotive's almost mystical ability to stand up to all kinds of punishment, the job does get done.

By the late 1960s, a motive power crisis was reached and following the withdrawal of some of the older Bagnalls after a long and arduous working life, it was declared that more engines were needed. Bagnalls had by this time closed down, and indeed steam building had virtually ceased all over the world. After investigating many possibilities, the answer to the problem was surprisingly found to lie close to Assam's border, where at Darjeeling, four of Sharp Stewart's celebrated B class 0–4–0STs stood condemned by the Darjeeling and Himalayan Railway. These were purchased at varying prices, and following extensive overhauls were put to work along with the Bagnalls. It was later intended to order three new boilers for the Bs from Calcutta, and assuming that work is currently in hand for these, this amazing outpost of British steam will continue.

The steam-worked collieries of the Assam Coalfield are Tipong, Namdang and Tirap. Tipong has an output of 750 tons per day and operates a three shift system through 24 hours. Motive power comprises B class 0-4-0STs, along with *Sally*, built as Bagnall's No. 2447 in 1930. Here the atmosphere is reminiscent of early industrial times in Britain, and one feels that time has stood still for over a century. Collieries and slag tips coexist with the workers' tiny dwellings, around which ragged children play, and animals abound. The valley seems shrouded in a permanent smoky haze, caused partly by the open coal fires of the dwellings. Smoking boiler house chimneys silhouette against the hills as the coals are raised by steam, and locomotive sounds day and night give piquancy to this industrial landscape.

Nearby are the coke ovens at Namdang, where *Rang Ring* is found. This delightful engine is decked in red livery, and was built as Bagnall's No. 1733 in May 1904. Although reduced in significance, Namdang's coke ovens still supply Calcutta.

At Tirap I found *David* (Bagnall's No. 2132 of 1924) and *Betty* (Bagnall's No. 2448 of 1931) at work, with *Queenie* (Bagnall's No. 2100 of 1919) under repair. Here the operations are centred upon open cast mining and the coal is taken away by road in fleets of multicoloured lorries festooned with fairy lights.

A brickworks was built at Ledo to service the collieries of the Assam field, and to this day, gangs of gaily dressed women hack the clay from the earth and, having loaded it into wicker baskets, manually fill the diminutive wagons of the waiting train. After several hours of such endeavour, the train makes its precarious way over rickety weed-strewn tracks to the brickworks, where a Manchester kiln is in use. Prior to depositing the clay at the works, the Bagnall has to surmount a gradient of 1 in 30 with seven loaded tubs, and in its endeavour the engine is aided by half a dozen labourers who help to heave the train over the top.

Ledo's main engine is No. 1556, an unnamed one of 1899; originally this engine was an 0-4-2, but over the intervening 80 years has lost her trailing axle and today runs on only four wheels. The standby engine at Ledo is No. 1437, one of the original two which Bagnall shipped for the Assam Railway and Trading Company in 1894.

Although the circumstances in Assam are unusual, it is nevertheless remarkable that this compact stud of Bagnalls should continue when most of their counterparts have perished. These engines have paid for themselves many times over, and despite their antiquity, still perform the job for which they were built. The Assam coalfield engines remain as living testimonials to the pride and skill which was Bagnall's hallmark in those glorious days before inbuilt obsolescence was invented.

Sally is a regular fire thrower, being fed on a mixture of wood shavings and slack. The muddy substance plastered around the smokebox door is cow dung and is used to prevent air leaking into the smokebox. Any such leaks would upset the engine's steaming capacity.

Overleaf: David draws a string of coal tubs from a hillside mine. Built by Bagnalls in 1924, *David* has lost his cab; he has also lost his couplings and has to pull his wagons with a chain. His boiler has grown weaker over the years and the pressure has been reduced accordingly. Today, *David* runs on only 90 p.s.i. and thus can pull just half the wagons he could in his prime.

6 High-Speed Thoroughbreds

Most people are fascinated by a high-speed steam train, and during the 1930s when services in Britain reached a peak, the public would flock to the lineside to watch such crack expresses as the *Coronation* or *Silver Jubilee* dash their way between London and Scotland. For Britain the true greyhound of steam was the Pacific 4–6–2. There were, of course, many other engines capable of high-speed running. Gooche's broad gauge 4–2–2s of the Great Western were allegedly running at speeds of up to 90 m.p.h. – 80 years before the Pacific was generally adopted – but for sustained running at high speed, the popular imagination was truly captured by the Pacific.

The 'golden age' of the British Pacific was from 1930 until 1960 and although the type's inherent stability combined with general improvements in locomotive design did much to facilitate sustained fast running, the Pacific was aided by superior track, signalling systems and braking. The prelude to the Pacific's flamboyance began with the inside-cylinder 4–4–0, the definitive express passenger type of the late Victorian and Edwardian period, when sustained speeds of better than one mile per minute became commonplace over certain sections. Indeed it was with such engines that a three-figure speed was reached for the first time, when the Great Western Railway's *City of Truro* made its epic 102-m.p.h. dash down Wellington Bank in 1904.

Around the turn of the century, train weights increased markedly; restaurant and sleeping cars were coming into widespread use whilst the coaching stock itself was becoming heavier. This led to rapid developments, for although the inside-cylinder 4–4–0 was pre-eminent, it was challenged by the Atlantic (4–4–2) and 4–6–0. The Atlantic heralded the Pacific by permitting a wide firebox which spread outwards over the rear axle thus increasing the capacity, to be incorporated. In contrast, the 4–4–0 and 4–6–0 had their firebox set between the frames, which restricted the capacity.

The inside-cylinder 4–4–0's role as an express passenger engine was paramount in British railway history. The type also featured in exports – usually to the 'more developed' countries where faster services were possible. Today, the last examples of this great dynasty are to be found working cross-country passenger trains in Pakistan. Here is Pakistan Railway's SPS class No. 2999. The first examples of her type were built by Beyer Peacock in 1904. These lovely engines are, in essence, typical Manchester locomotives and are very similar to the Manchester Sheffield and Lincolnshire Railway's 4–4–0s designed during the 1890s by Henry Pollitt.

The equation between narrow and wide fireboxes depended upon the quality of coal available. This fact was clearly demonstrated by the Great Western, who remained with the four-cylinder 4–6–0 because of the superior quality of Welsh coal, and their King class 4–6–0 had the same tractive effort as an L.M.S. Princess Royal Pacific, although its grate area was only 34 sq. ft., compared with the 41 sq. ft. of the Pacific.

The Pacific was able to work heavy trains in excess of 500 tons on start-to-stop timings of one mile per minute, although in its high-speed exploits the trains were rather more moderately loaded. The closest challenge in terms of sheer speed came from the Great Western Railway's four-cylinder 4–6–0 Castle class. During the 1930s these engines worked the *Cheltenham Flyer*, dubbed as the world's fastest train, and booked to cover the 77.2 miles from Swindon to Paddington in 65 minutes.

The steam greyhound, whatever its type, was a highly specialised machine with a shorter life span than any other form of locomotive. Sustained fast running with heavy trains was the most stressful of all duties, and the most vulnerable to displacement in that constant quest for more speed and power which overshadowed every express design. Once displaced from the top duties, alternative employment was difficult to find for powerful 4–6–0s or Pacifics. On lesser work, they were either uneconomic or too heavy on the axle, whilst for slow heavy pulling their large driving wheels – which were built for speed – rendered them totally unsuitable.

It was the greyhound's inability to adapt to other work which has rendered it almost extinct today. In Britain, all disappeared rapidly once other forms of motive power took over, and much the same has happened abroad. At this point however, a fundamental distinction must be made, for the high-speed steam train as Britain knew it was never exported. Certainly we sent 4–4–0s, 4–6–0s and Pacifics in various combinations to many countries, but nowhere did they approach the best of the home performances. Outside Britain, the high-speed steam train was a phenomenon of the most industrially advanced nations, U.S.A., France, Germany, etc., countries which built their own locomotives.

The rarity of the high-speed thoroughbred is thus emphasised by the fact that few of the world's railways were capable of running such trains. Almost all of Africa was laid with gauges of 3 ft. 6 in. or less, as were large areas of Latin America and Asia. Such gauges were invariably built through rough country with many curves and gradients, but even when the terrain was suitable, the narrow gauges rendered really fast running impossible.

One country which did receive superb express passenger designs from Britain was Argentina, many of whose lines were laid by British engineers to the 5 ft. 6 in.-gauge. The country took 4–4–0s, 4–6–0s and Pacifics of classic British delineation. The first 4–6–0s appeared during the early years of the century, and by 1927, three-cylinder Pacifics were in operation. These Pacifics had 6 ft. 6 in.-diameter driving wheels, and worked 800-ton trains from Buenos Aires to Bahia Blanca on the Atlantic Coast. The class was named after historic members of Argentina's armed forces. The ultimate Argentinian Pacifics appeared in 1948 with a class of 40 three-cylinder examples with 6 ft. 3 in.-diameter driving wheels and Caprotti valve gear.

Argentina's expresses were less frequent and thus heavier than their British counterparts. Speeds were generally lower, but sustained dashes of 70 m.p.h. were often achieved over the flat fertile pampas lands, and this was possibly the closest ever reached to the traditions of the mother country. Although displaced from service, examples of Argentina's 4–6–0s and Pacifics can still be found lying out of use, and one example would make a worthy exhibit in the proposed new museum discussed in Chapter 2.

The other major recipient of traditional British express passenger power was India, which until 1947 was under British rule. If any country mirrored the colour and variety of Britain's railways, it was those of the Indian subcontinent. Right up to independence, the vast majority of locomotives came from Britain, and followed the British concept in virtually every respect. In fact, so great was the diversity, that a set of standard designs was prepared for the 5 ft. 6 in.-gauge lines with the help of the British Engineers Standards Association (B.E.S.A.). Under this scheme, inside-cylinder 4–4–0, Atlantic 4–4–2 and 4–6–0 express and mail engines appeared, and were almost indistinguishable from the types of engines that were being built in Britain. Today, examples of the 4–4–0s can still be found in Pakistan, whilst an updated version of the 4–6–0 remains active in India – the last examples having been built as recently as 1951.

The age of the Pacific locomotive in India coincided with that in Britain, as during the 1920s five new standard designs were prepared for the 5 ft. 6 in.-gauge lines. Known as the X series, three were Pacifics, the XA, XB and XC. The XA was a light Pacific for use on secondary lines only, and may be disregarded in the present context, but the XB and XC were intended for fast, heavy trains. The largest was the XC which had a firegrate area of 51 sq. ft. in order to consume the poorer grades of Bengali coal.

Exciting in appearance, these designs resemble the L.N.E.R. Pacifics, which were all the rage in Britain during the 1920s, although the Indian engines were two-cylinder as opposed to Gresley's being three-cylinder. Unfortunately, they did not rise to expectations; problems arose with steaming, frame fractures and firebox tubeplates, but the most serious was instability when running at speed. It was this last factor which most worried the authorities, and following the Bihta accident on the East Indian Railway in 1937, a committee – which included William Stanier and E. S. Cox of the L.M.S. – was sent from England the following year to investigate the Pacifics.

Modifications were made and the engines improved to do some superb work, and in certain areas to be actually revered, but they were never really trusted at speed, and 60 m.p.h. has been regarded as the outer limit ever since. When considering the brilliance of Britain's Pacifics at home, it is sad that the XCs should have incurred such problems; nevertheless they have outlived their British counterparts by many years.

It will be seen from the foregoing, that the handsome British greyhound was in world terms a rare beast, and today borders upon extinction. No traces of the brief but highly elegant Atlantic era survive, the only Atlantics in existence being in Mozambique, but these were never intended for fast running. One vestige of the streamlined era exists in the now abandoned Iraqi Pacifics exported from Robert Stephenson and Hawthorn's works in 1941. These engines had driving wheels of only 5 ft. 9 in. diameter, and were not built for undue speed, 60 m.p.h. being about the maximum permitted. Exactly why they were built in fully streamlined form remains one of the puzzles of latter-day British locomotive practice.

Had the home tradition survived, the Pacific would have lead to the 4–6–4, which only occurred with Gresley's solitary W1. Logically the 4–8–4 would have been next in succession. Both types appeared in export packages, and especially notable were the 70 4–6–4 express engines shipped to Australia during the 1950s.

The first 4–8–4s went out much earlier with the 24 192-ton giants built by the Vulcan Foundry during the 1930s for the Chinese National Railways. One of these historic engines was recently repatriated and now resides in the National Railway Museum in York.

During the 1950s the North British works in Glasgow built the mighty 25 class condensing and non-condensing 4–8–4s for the South African Railways. Both the Chinese and South African examples were potentially very fast runners and the condensers, were often paced at 70 m.p.h., albeit that their 3 ft. 6 in.-gauge caused·them to be restricted to an official 60 m.p.h.

With this in mind, recent developments in South Africa can

only be described as amazing, as in 1980 plans were announced to rebuild a 25 class 4–8–4 non-condensing engine into a new 26 class. The engine selected was No. 3450, and the rebuild incorporated many technical developments based partly around the wonderful work done over recent years by the famous Argentinian steam engineer L. D. Porta, after whom it was appropriately named.

Nicknamed 'the Red Devil', she is the world's most modern steam locomotive, and my reason for including her here is that Mr. D. Wardale who supervised the rebuilding and subsequent road tests, has recently been reported as saying that No. 3450 could – if permitted – break the world speed record for steam of 126 m.p.h. set by Gresley's A4 Pacific *Mallard* in 1938. However one evaluates such a claim, it provides a stimulating and heartening thought for the 1980s.

Overleaf: The last surviving Indian Railway's XB Pacific No. 22153 (Vulcan Foundry 1927) crosses the viaduct at Rajamundry with a stopping train from Eluru. These Pacifics formed part of the X series standards for India's 5 ft.-6 in.-gauge lines and 99 were built between 1927 and 1931 for medium-range express work.

Left: A detailed study of XB No. 22153 showing the fine greyhound-like appearance which characterised most British Pacific designs. It was my privilege to work with this engine as she ended her days working local passenger trains around the Godavi Delta in Andhra Pradesh.

Overleaf: The last surviving XC Pacific No. 22224 approaches Bolpur with the daily pick up freight from Burdwan. It was on this humble duty in Bengal that this last greyhound of British steam ended its days. She was built by the Vulcan Foundry, Lancashire in 1929.

Left: This thoroughbred of British 4–6–0s complete with 6 ft.-diameter wheels originally worked on the British owned 5 ft.-6 in.-gauge Buenos Aires and Great Southern Railway, or BAGS as it was affectionately known in Argentina. Classified 12 A, she was originally a two-cylinder compound having been built by Beyer Peacock in 1906. After withdrawal from main-line service, she was purchased by the naval authorities for shunting supplies around a base on the Atlantic Coast.

Above: The daily pick up freight from Burdwan to Bolpur was one of the last main-line duties for the XCs during the final years of their working life. They were regular performers on this train for many years until their final demise in 1981 and their appearance 'on line' had all the atmosphere and mystique of a once famous, but now rare, thoroughbred ekeing out its days.

Here we see No. 22216 – also a Vulcan Foundry engine of 1929 – with a full train on a sharp winter's morning in 1976.

7 Garratts and other Articulateds

Following the demise of the British Pacific the popular imagination has been captured by the Garratt. Even people not generally interested in railways have heard of the giants which bend on curves and have their boilers slung between the wheels. There has been much in the national media – both television and press – concerning Garratts in Africa, not least Zimbabwe's recent decision to overhaul large numbers of them for a return to mainline operation. If these lumbering brontosauruses of the locomotive world fascinate the layman, it is hardly surprising that they are amongst the most sought after type by enthusiasts, and package tours for railfans from all over the world have been visiting South Africa and Zimbabwe, two of the leading countries which use Garratts.

Although the Garratt is an entirely British concept, it is perhaps surprising that so few ever worked on the home railways. Only one significant class emerged when the L.M.S. took delivery of 33 2–6–0 + 0–6–2s during the late 1920s, for working heavy trains between the Nottinghamshire coalfield and London. These Garratts alleviated the double heading of older 0–6–0s, and proved themselves to be superb haulers. Despite a working life of some 30 years however, the L.M.S. Garratts were not the most popular of engines with their crews. The Garratt phase was never repeated in Britain, and the 2–8–0 became regarded as adequate for an overall policy of frequent 'medium-sized' freight hauls.

The Garratt represents the last important evolutionary advance in articulated steam traction, the need for which had been felt since the early years of locomotive development. A principal early form was the Fairlie, which consisted of two locomotives placed back to back but with a common central firebox which could be built to large proportions. Under this arrangement, each locomotive was carried on bogies. The driver occupied one side of the central cab, and the fireman the other. The Fairlie saw service in many parts of the world, and was a genuine articulated, which gave the power of two locomotives but required only one crew.

In contrast, the Meyer was in effect a large tank engine mounted on twin power bogies with the cylinders grouped at the inner ends of each bogie, in order that the steam feed pipe from the dome should be as short as possible. The Meyer possessed the disadvantage of having its firebox above the wheels, so restricting its depth, but it gained on the Fairlie in having a normal situation for the crew, and an infinitely superior fuel carrying capacity.

The Meyer's disadvantage of a restricted firebox was solved by Kitson of Leeds, who spread the bogies further apart, and set the firebox between them. In this arrangement, the cylinders were often placed at the outer ends of each bogie, and in many cases the steam from the rear cylinders passed through the rear water tank, and was exhausted through a separate chimney. The Kitson Meyer constituted an excellent articulated locomotive, but its evolutionary advance was largely cut short by the Garratt, which was vastly superior.

The Mallet represented a very different concept in which the boiler was mounted on a normal frame, but joined to the front of which was a form of pony truck which carried the leading set of cylinders and wheels, whilst the rear set remained fixed. The first Mallet appeared during the 1880s when a Frenchman named Anatole Mallet devised a four-cylinder compound tank engine of 60cm. gauge. His principle however, was suitable for either tank or tender engines – compound or simple – and the Mallet was destined to grow rapidly in size. Its diversity ranged from small plantation tank engines to the giant tender engines of North America, which culminated in the Union Pacific's 520-ton Big Boys.

The Mallet was by far the most numerous articulated type, and the most varied in its application. Traditionally it was a four-cylinder compound in contrast with the Garratt, which was a four-cylinder simple. During the later years of development, the Mallet became associated with North America whilst the Garratt found its greatest favour in Africa.

The Garratt was conceived by H. W. Garratt, an Englishman who was born in 1864. Having served his apprenticeship at Bow Works, Garratt was employed as a locomotive engineer in many countries. He achieved first-hand experience of several articulated locomotive types, as such engines were becoming increasingly prevalent amid the rough terrain of the world at large. Having conceived his principle, Garratt touted it around a number of Britain's private locomotive builders, and eventually succeeded in convincing Beyer Peacock of its merit. Having patented his idea in 1907, Garratt granted Beyer Peacock the sole British manufacturing rights on a royalty basis. Thus was born the now legendary Beyer Garratt.

On a Garratt engine the boiler and firebox were free of axles and so could be built to whatever size was needed, both for ample generation of steam and proper combustion of gases by the provision of a deep firebox. Conversely, as the wheels were free of the boiler they could be made to whatever diameter was considered best. By placing the engine's wheels and cylinders under a front water unit and rear coal unit, situated either side of the boiler, the engine's weight was spread over a wide area. Then, simply by articulating these two units from the boiler, a large powerful locomotive, capable of moving heavy loads over curved, graded and lightly laid lines, could be built.

Britain's colonial markets ensured that Garratts spread to many parts of the world where they were eminently suited to rugged terrain and difficult operating conditions. As countries became increasingly industrialised, heavier demands were made upon the railways and under such circumstances the Garratt increasingly came into its own.

Britain had the largest number of main-line Garratts in Europe, Spain being the only other notable recipient. The largest Garratt ever built went to Russia, a country not normally associated with the type. This solitary giant with a 20-ton axle loading was designed to haul 2,500-ton trains, but the type was not perpetuated. India, New Zealand, South America and particularly Australia were all Garratt users.

Garratts will always be associated with the African continent. From Algeria and Sudan in the north, East Africa, Angola and Zimbabwe in the central area, through to Mozambique and South Africa, the Garratt has seen extensive operation. Many exciting classes have been produced for working throughout these regions, principally for slogging freight hauls, but also for passenger duties. Whether it be on tortuous climbs inland over the steep coastal escarpments, or amid the interior where the rough landscape causes the track beds to undulate like corrugated iron, the African Garratt performs supremely.

Being a product of the twentieth century and a major variant on the conventional steam locomotive, it might appear strange that the Garratt has not seen wider use. Certainly the oft-stated theory that steam had been developed to its ultimate potential within permissible loading gauges, thus heralding a necessity for an alternate form of motive power, can easily be refuted, owing to the enormous possibilities for expansion within the Garratt concept. South Africa has done greatest justice to the type ever since its introduction there in 1919. For all the inherent possibilities, it seems ironic that less than 2,000 Garratts were ever built, though perhaps the best epitaph for them is the fact that a good percentage are still in operation.

The distinction of having the greatest dependence upon Garratts must, however, go to nearby Zimbabwe where 150 of them, embracing four different classes, constitute some 95 per cent of the country's highly utilised steam fleet. It is still the Manchester-built Garratt which takes the huge coal hauls across Zimbabwe, from the Wankie coalfield near the Zambian border, into Bulawayo. This work is partly undertaken by the ultimate in Zimbabwean steam traction – the 95 ft.-long 20th class 4–8–2 + 2–8–4, built between 1954 and 1958. By 1975, Bulawayo possessed the world's largest Garratt operation, since the majority of Zimbabwe's steam engines are now concentrated there. Imagine walking through the depot with some 70 enormous Garratts looming up on all sides, the tremendous aura of power, and hardly a conventional engine in sight. Such a scene could hardly have been imagined when H. W. Garratt first called upon Beyer Peacock to discuss his idea for an articulated engine nearly 80 years ago.

Fortunately the first Garratt ever built – a 2 ft. 0 in.-gauge 0–4–0 + 0–4–0 for the Tasmania Railway in 1909 – has now been returned to Britain for preservation, and can be found on the Festiniog where amazingly the Garratt's early ancestor the Fairlie not only worked, one and a quarter centuries ago, but also exists under preservation there today.

Although the Fairlie and Garratt were adopted on a limited scale in Britain, neither the Mallet or Kitson Meyer ever appeared. Although all four featured in export packages, only the Garratt remains in evidence today, despite the fact that as recently as the 1950s, Bagnall of Stafford built some Mallet tanks for plantation work in South Africa.

It used to be said that the Garratt, though fascinating, was a visual desecration of the steam locomotive's conventional form. But the Garratt is in its own right an extremely handsome machine – albeit an acquired taste. A few weeks amongst them in Africa would soon prove their considerable aesthetical merit.

A mighty GMA class 4–8–2 + 2–8–4 Garratt of the South African Railways storms a 1 in 37 gradient in Natal. South Africa was the biggest user of Garratts and the GMAs – built in Britain and Germany between 1952/8 – originally numbered 120 engines.

With an axle weight of less than 15 tons and a tractive effort of 68,000 lbs, the GMAs were ideal for almost every type of operation. In order to reduce the axle loading to a minimum, a separate water tank of 6,750 gallons capacity is carried behind the locomotive.

This vintage
2–8–2 + 2–8–2 Garratt,
caught working at the
Transvaal Navigation
Colliery in South Africa,
was originally delivered
to the Rhodesian Railways
as their 16th class No. 609
in 1938. The Rhodesian
16s first appeared in 1929
and were able to lift 700-
ton trains over 1 in 40
gradients. Although
Zimbabwe remains a big
Garratt user, all the 16s
have been withdrawn,
but several were sold to
collieries in neighbouring
South Africa to fulfil the
role of industrial steam
superpower.

Above: The biggest steam locomotives left in the world are the Kenyan Railway's Mountain class 4–8–2 + 2–8–4 Garratts, 34 of which were built by Beyer Peacock in 1955. Named after the highest mountains of East Africa, these metre-gauge giants weighed 250 tons in full working order. They worked between Mombasa and Nairobi – a distance of 332 miles – and here is No. 5922 *Mount Blackett* climbing the Mombasa spiral.

Right: Like a rediscovered dodo, the last surviving Kitson Meyer hauls a demolition train over the metals of Chile's Taltal railway, built for hauling nitrates from the Atacama Desert to the Pacific Coast. Built by Kitson of Leeds during the Edwardian period, this 0–6–6–0 was one of many similar engines which operated on the British-owned nitrate railways of Chile. The centre plume of steam is issuing from the safety valves whilst the right-hand one is the exhaust from the rear pair of cylinders.

8 Freight Locomotives: the Homespun Variety (Duck 6s-Decapods)

The British freight locomotive went through remarkably few phases during its one and a quarter centuries of evolution. Dominant throughout was the inside-cylinder 0–6–0 which first appeared during the 1830s, and continued to be built in basically unchanged form for over a century, the last examples being Bulleid's Q1s for the Southern Railway in 1942. Known in its later years as the Duck 6, the inside-cylinder 0–6–0 was built in thousands, and from the middle of the nineteenth century it appeared with virtually every railway company and assumed innumerable different designs. Although some inside-cylinder 0–6–0s were officially designated as mixed traffics, the type was predominantly a freight hauler, and up until the late 1950s, could still be seen heading sizeable freight trains over main-line networks.

The 0–6–0's utility was evidenced by its relatively short wheelbase which enabled it to negotiate curves. The type also had an excellent factor of adhesion as the engine's full weight was applied to the driving wheels. The relative stability of the track in Britain enabled goods engines to work without pony trucks or bogies, whilst another key factor in the 0–6–0's continued usage was the high quality of British coal. This permitted use of small fireboxes which in the case of the 0–6–0 was tucked between the engine's frames in front of the rear coupled axle.

Although the inside-cylinder 0–6–0 might be regarded as the definitive British steam locomotive, it was primarily a home phenomenon and did not appear extensively in exports, as the operating conditions in most countries demanded locomotives with additional carrying axles for stability.

By far the greatest deployment of inside-cylinder 0–6–0s overseas was on the 5 ft. 6 in.-gauge lines of the Indian subcontinent. Considerable numbers were shipped out during the late nineteenth century and some classic British examples were actually built at the Jamalpur works in Northern India from 1899

One of the last British inside-cylinder 0–6–0s left in the world ends its days as works pilot locomotive at Jamalpur on India's Eastern Railway. This veteran is one of a handful of survivors representing India's century-long association with this, the 'definitive' form of British locomotive.

onwards. But the type was truly expanded when it formed one of the seven standard designs for India under the B.E.S.A. programme of 1903. Under this scheme many Indian 5 ft. 6 in.-gauge systems were recipients and building continued until the 1920s when the B.E.S.A. designs were superseded by the X series discussed in the following chapter.

On Britain's home railways the 0–8–0 had appeared well before the turn of the century. Continued industrial expansion inevitably meant that mineral trains were becoming heavier, and the 0–8–0 was in principle an enlarged 0–6–0 with more power and adhesion. Again the 0–8–0 proved ideal for slow and slogging hauls over stable trackbeds in Britain, but very few were exported and whilst it was consolidating its position on the home railways, Britain's private builders were exporting the more stable 2–8–0, and in so doing were anticipating Britain's domestic needs from the Edwardian period onwards.

As Britain's railway network became increasingly utilised, it was inevitable that the sluggishness of the 0–6–0/0–8–0 would cause busy lines to become cluttered with long slow-moving freights. The advent of the 2–8–0 with its leading pony truck heralded a more lively movement of goods trains, and following its introduction on Britain's main lines in 1903, the type set the theme for the following half century and was only just usurped by the 2–10–0 before steam development finished altogether. Thus it will be seen that the 0–6–0, 0–8–0 and 2–8–0 fulfilled virtually all Britain's home needs. The good trackbeds, moderate loads and frequency of service combined with the availability of high calorific coal demanded nothing larger.

Unlike most 0–6–0s and 0–8–0s, the 2–8–0 had its cylinder placed outside. Throughout its evolution it was primarily a two-cylinder machine, and whether built for home or world service, it maintained a highly characteristic and typically British shape. Apart from forming part of the B.E.S.A. scheme for India's 5 ft. 6 in.-gauge lines, the 2–8–0 saw widespread service with examples exported to such diverse places as Australia, Egypt, Argentina, Peru and China. In common with the 0–6–0, the 2–8–0 was prolifically used abroad in both world wars, and although most of the indigenous examples were either returned to Britain or subsequently broken up, Stanier 8F 2–8–0s remain active in Turkey whilst abandoned ones exist in Iraq and Iran, nations embroiled in a drawn out war.

The last major class of 2–8–0 exported by Britain was the famous United Nations Relief and Rehabilitation Association (U.N.R.R.A.) Liberations. Introduced in 1946, all came from the Vulcan Foundry although representatives of seven European countries were involved in the design. This class of engines was intended for service in liberated countries following World War 2, and they worked in Luxembourg, Poland, Czechoslovakia and Yugoslavia.

As might be imagined, the Liberations broke away from the traditional concept of the handsome British 2–8–0, and although they had plate frames, their firebox and footplating were set well above the driving wheels. In short, they were a utilitarian design of rather Americanised appearance and were a perfect example of the changing shape of British locomotives – whether for home or export – in the years following World War 2. This was a period when engines the world over began to assume an international appearance which had more of an American flavour than many observers would have liked.

However, World War 2 did create one precedent which indirectly heralded the final evolutionary strain of British freight engines. That precedent was the introduction of the first 2–10–0. Surprisingly, the intention was to achieve a light axle load rather than greater power, and the engines concerned were a ten-coupled version of the Austerity 2–8–0. Most of these Decapods went abroad in war service and derelict examples survive in Greece and Syria. Following the nationalisation of Britain's railways in 1948, 12 standard designs were prepared for the entire country, and amongst them was the 9F class 2–10–0. This time the emphasis was not upon a light axle loading but a heavy mineral engine in its own right with a tractive effort of some 40,000 lbs. Thus the evolution of the British goods engine had at the eleventh hour aspired to ten-coupled traction.

Britain's gravitation to the 2–10–0 was, of course, many years after its adoption in other parts of the world, and one cannot help but compare the 9F with that other *pièce de résistance* of British freight engines, the L.M.S.'s four-cylinder Garratts of 1927. Although the Garratt was more powerful, it had an axle loading of 21 tons compared with the mere $15\frac{1}{2}$ tons of a 9F. For British conditions the 9F represented the ultimate that was deemed necessary and with it, development of the British freight locomotive ended.

It is perhaps surprising that the 2–10–0 was not featured extensively in British export packages, but many of the developing countries did need the greater flexibility of the types mentioned in the following chapter. One significant example however is the Turkish State Railway's 56 class, 15 of which were built by Beyer Peacock in 1948. However, these engines are almost entirely German in design and appearance and they represent the only ten-coupled locomotives ever built by Beyer Peacock.

Left: In common with the inside-cylinder 0−6−0, the 2−8−0 also featured extensively in Britain's 1903 standard locomotive scheme for India. Although standard designs were envisaged, the various railway companies invariably requested detail variations and this engine is the last survivor of the South Eastern Railway's HSM class. The HSMs were formerly the main-line freight haulers for the Bengal and Nagpur Railway and here No. 26190 is depicted in her original B & N livery. She was built by Armstrong Whitworth of Newcastle upon Tyne in 1924.

Above: The Stanier 8Fs which survive on the Turkish State railways have captured the imagination of most British railway enthusiasts. In this scene at Irmak Junction we see No. 45161, built by North British in 1941, taking a break between shunting duties. The 8F is uncharacteristically decked with a cowcatcher and Westinghouse brake pumps but an aura of nostalgia prevails in her superb 'Willesden grey' livery!

Left: In contrast with the SCR's HSM class, No. 26761 is more typically decked in latter day 'nationalisation grime'. This engine belongs to the Eastern Railway's HGS class and was delivered to the East Indian Railway in 1920 from William Beardmore's works at Dalmuir on the Clyde.

Overleaf: 'Mixed freight to Fray Bentos.' This scene in Uruguay depicts the sole remaining T class 2–8–0 No. 139 *Ing Pedro Magnou* preparing to head a goods train along the line which leads to this famous meat canning port on the River Plate. This lovely 2–8–0 is very similar to the type of engine one would have found in the Scottish Highlands during the 1920s. She is named after a famous Uruguayan engineer.

97

Britain was many years behind America and Europe in turning to the 2–10–0 and did not do so until this design was introduced by Riddles for War Department service in 1943. Only one other class of British 2–10–0 followed and the epoch ended in 1968 when British Railways' final steam locomotives were withdrawn. Fortunately examples of the W.D. variety continued to work in Syria and Greece well into the 1970s and here we see one of the Greek examples on standby duty at Alexandropolis.

9 Freight Locomotives: Export Variety (Mikados – Confederations)

We have seen that Britain with its high calorific value coal, strong trackbeds with relatively easy gradient profiles and policy of frequent, moderately loaded trains, seldom needed anything larger than the 2–8–0. This rather idyllic situation was in marked contrast to the conditions prevailing in the rough and tumble of the world at large, where railways had to be laid cheaply in countries whose industrial potential had not been developed. Invariably gauges were smaller than standard, and many lines abounded in tight curves, gradients and frail bridges. Available coal was often inferior to the British variety, and the high clinker content played havoc in engines not designed for such conditions.

It was around the turn of the century when building of the world's railways was sufficiently advanced that the divergence of types began, and whilst Britain moved towards the 0–8–0 the exporters were designing and building the 4–8–0 which was one of the earliest departures from home practice. In common with many of Britain's 'export variety' freight locomotives, development occurred initially in the United States, where the 4–8–0 was in regular use well before the end of the nineteenth century, having to some extent replaced the ubiquitous 4–4–0. Britain's first example was built during the 1890s when Dubs of Glasgow built the 7th class 4–8–0 for South Africa's Cape Government Railway. This created a precedent for the type in Africa and it spread throughout the continent, often with designs similar to the Cape engines. The 4–8–0 could take a larger boiler than the 2–8–0 for the same axle load whilst the bogie provided vital stability. Britain produced more 4–8–0s than any other country, and no less than 17 different builders were involved.

The 4–8–0 either had its firebox placed between the coupled axles or immediately above them and was therefore limited in its size. Following America's pioneering of the wide firebox around the turn of the century, the 2–8–2 Mikado became prevalent. The

The British three-cylinder 4–8–0 was an exciting engine by any standards and here is the last survivor of the Argentinian 11c class, the first of which was exhibited at the Wembley Exhibition in 1924. A total of 75 were exported to Argentina where they worked trains of up to 2,000 tons. Their building in Britain followed the introduction of Gresley's three-cylinder 2–8–0s for the Great Northern Railway.

use of a trailing axle enabled the firebox to be built deeper and to spread outwards – a facility which was invaluable when dealing with poorer coal. Certainly the 4–8–0 was less likely to slip when pulling heavy loads, but the 2–8–2 permitted larger coupled wheels – within a given loading gauge – and was generally regarded as a faster engine. In America alone some 14,000 Mikados are said to have run.

Though hardly used at all on Britain's home railways, the Mikado was exported prolifically for over half a century, particularly to nations in Africa and Asia. As early as 1903, the North British Works of Glasgow were building the type for heavy freight work in South Africa.

Perhaps the best known British Mikados were those included in the Indian Railway's Standards (I.R.S.) prepared for the subcontinent during the 1920s. On the 5 ft. 6 in.-gauge lines these included the XD for lighter freight hauls, and the far larger XE heavy mineral design. In contrast, the YDs for the metre-gauge lines provided an excellent mixed traffic design.

The 2–8–2 was to see infinitely more widespread use in India when the I.R.S. designs were followed by American designs during World War 2. Shortly after independence, India received the first of the all pervading WG class 2–8–2s which eventually totalled 2,450 engines. The first 100 WGs were built in Britain but many were subsequently built at India's Chittaranjan works. The WGs were the largest class built for any Commonwealth railway.

The Mikado was almost universally a two-cylinder concept, but in 1925 the Vulcan Foundry played an exciting variation on the theme when they produced a class of massive three-cylinder examples for Nigeria. What a comparison these giants made with their British counterparts – the inside-cylinder 0–6–0, or on the more progressive railways the two-cylinder 2–8–0! In the post-war years, Nigeria continued to use the Mikado with their famous River class which was later adapted for the countries of the East African Railways Corporation – Kenya, Tanzania and Uganda – where the type became known as Tribals. Amongst the last Mikados to be built in Britain were the ubiquitous 141F class engines for Spain.

The next evolutionary stage was the 4–8–2 which might be thought of as an upgraded 2–8–2, but with better tracking facilities. Known as the Mountain, the type was developed in America both for passenger and freight work, but those which Britain exported were – in the early years at least – for gauges less than standard.

The principal recipient of British 4–8–2s was South Africa, where many routes are lightly laid and steeply graded. Under such conditions the 4–8–2's combination of power and flexibility proved ideal and from the Edwardian period onwards South Africa took large numbers of Mountains from the British builders. Notable amongst the early designs was the 12th class built for hauling heavy trains over the Witbank coalfield in the Transvaal. With a tractive effort of almost 40,000 lbs, the 12s were indeed giants for their day. Other designs followed and the 4–8–2 in various guises was to become the principal all-round engine of the Republic.

However, from 1925 onwards the South African 4–8–2 owed much to American practice following the introduction of the huge 15CBs from Baldwins of Philadelphia in 1926. All subsequent 4–8–2s supplied from Britain incorporated the American characteristics. The culmination was the 15F of which 255 were built – the most numerous class ever to work on the African continent. Most of this class was built by North British of Glasgow. Other British-built 4–8–2s worked in neighbouring Zimbabwe in addition to Ghana and Sudan.

One of the most memorable of British 4–8–2s was sent to New Zealand immediately before the outbreak of World War 2. These were the 40 semi-streamlined J class from North British. These magnificent engines built at the height of the streamlined era, came complete with Vanderbilt type tenders and were one of the most exciting designs ever exported from Britain.

The logical development of the 4–8–2 was, of course, the 4–8–4 which established itself in America during the 1920s. The effect upon British building practice was rapid, for in 1936 the Vulcan Foundry built 24 massive 4–8–4s for the Chinese National Railways. These were huge engines by any standards and they made a marked contrast with the Pacifics, which were the ultimate in motive power for the home networks. The Chinese 4–8–4s recently came back into the limelight when one was returned to Britain for preservation.

Although the Chinese engines were primarily for passenger workings, they created the precedent for the 4–8–4 in Britain, and almost 20 years later were followed by two classes for South Africa. Built between 1953 and 1954 these engines were the ultimate non-articulated motive power for the Republic. One of the designs consisted of a class of condensing engines built for working across the Karroo Desert, whilst the other was a conventional non-condensing variation. Classed as 25C and 25NC, building was in both cases shared between North British of Glasgow and Henschel of Germany.

The condensers could run for 700 miles without taking water, and they revolutionised services across the Karroo on the main line northwards from the Cape Province. Despite their gauge of 3 ft. 6 in. they were larger than any of Britain's domestic designs;

they had a grate area of 70 sq. ft., a tractive effort of 51,410 lbs., they were 107 ft. long, and in full working order weighed 234 tons!

The non-condensing variant was, in effect, a development of the previously mentioned 15F class. These also proved to be superb engines and they remain hard at work today, especially on the busy main line between Kimberley and De Aar.

The 2–8–4 – or Berkshire – came between the Mikado and Mountain and was able to combine the often needed virtues of a large grate area in addition to a very low axle weight. Thus Berkshires were ideal for difficult branch lines with infrequent but heavy trains in areas devoid of good coal. In 1949–50 North British built 100 Berkshires for South Africa where they ran on 45-lb. track, particularly in South West Africa.

The other notable British Berkshires were the East African Railway's 30/31 Tribal classes, which were built during the 1950s by North British and the Vulcan Foundry. These classes were a light-axle variant of the 29 class Tribal 2–8–2 and had a four-wheel Delta truck under the firebox. The Berkshire's utility is evidenced by the 31's 30-sq.-ft. grate area, and tractive effort of 26,600 lbs. for an axle load of only $11\frac{1}{2}$ tons. The only deficiency with so light a loading was that great care had to be taken when starting heavy trains to avoid serious bouts of slipping. Inevitably the Berkshire was pioneered in America where quite apart from axle weight considerations, the type evolved with truly massive fireboxes which fanned out way above the carrying truck.

As the 2–8–0 progressed to the 2–8–2, the 2–10–0 evolved into the 2–10–2 or Santa Fe. In 1939 Beyer Peacock received an order for 24 three-cylinder 2–10–2s for the Iranian State Railways, but the advent of World War 2 prevented their construction. After the war Beyer Peacock subcontracted this order to the Vulcan Foundry who, in the event, built the engines with only two cylinders.

In America, the Santa Fe provided a natural stepping stone to the Texas type 2–10–4. Here was American steam superpower; brutish engines with massive boilers and furnaces and enormous tractive efforts. As far as British builders were concerned the Texas type defined the limits, and none were ever built.

It will be seen that a large range of engines were built for export by the private foundries, often incorporating advanced technology in their designs, and it is amazing that these exerted so small an influence on the home railways. Britain's railways managed for better or worse with a highly characteristic range of engines of moderately sized proportions, drawn from a limited segment of the wheel arrangement spectrum.

Following America's lead, the wide firebox appeared early in Britain's locomotive exports, especially those bound for the African countries. A typical example was the Rhodesian Railway's 12A class 4–8–2. Here is No. 190, built by North British in 1926, heading a freight train to Wankie.

One of the mainstays of Indian motive power over the last half century has been the British XD class 2–8–2. Sadly these fine engines are now being withdrawn from service but some remain active particularly on the South Central Railway. Here we see No. 22372 – a North British engine of 1946 originally built for the Nizam's State Railway – at the head of a coal train from the Singareni Mines to Dornakal Junction.

This extremely handsome 4–8–0 is one of 30 two-cylinder examples exported to Argentina from the Vulcan Foundry in 1949 as an updated version of the earlier 15A 4–8–0s. Known as the 15Bs, they were excellent mixed-traffic engines but gained especial distinction on the seasonal fruit traffic over the 750-mile run from the Rio Negro Valley to Buenos Aires. On this duty they worked 1,000-ton loads on passenger train timings.

Overleaf: One of the largest industrial engines in the world is the South African Railway's 12A type seen here at the head of a coal train from Landau Colliery up to the connection with the main-line network. Descended from a main-line design of 1919, 12As were built in unsuperheated form for industrial service. This giant has a cylinder diameter of 24 in. and a tractive effort of 47,420 lbs.

Left: Very few Berkshires were exported from Britain and the most significant were the 100 examples built by North British in 1949/50 for running on 45-lb. track in South West Africa. Nowadays they work in South Africa and for many years have held sway on the George – Knysna branch in Cape Province, a duty which takes them over the famous Kaaiman's River Bridge with the Indian Ocean in the background.

Overleaf: With its turbines whirring, a South African Railway's 25 condensing class 4–8–4 eases its train back onto the main line after being looped in the Karroo Desert. Possibly the only condensing engines left in the world, these 235-ton giants can run for 700 miles without taking water and their introduction into the arid Karroo enabled many of the cumbersome 'watering stations' to be abandoned.

10 Tank Engines Galore

Of the million or so steam locomotives that are believed to have been built it is possible that one third were tank engines. The tank engine breaks down into four basic spheres of operation: industrial, suburban, branch and shunting. In order to follow their evolution and present day status, it is preferable to discuss each group separately.

Industrial tanks

The first industrial tank engine appeared almost one and a half centuries ago in the form of contractor's engines used by the railway builders during the frenzied construction of the 1840s/50s. These builders required a compact and economical engine, light enough to work over hastily laid tracks, able to negotiate tight curves, and yet have sufficient adhesion to draw heavy train-loads of earth and materials. Additionally, the engines needed to be easy to transport from one site to another, and small tank engines were the obvious answer. Commensurate with this great period of railway building came the rapid development of collieries, quarries and foundries along with other industrial establishments, and these sites, which rapidly became linked to the main railway network, also demanded their own locomotives. The contractor's tank provided an ideal basis, and by 1850 the industrial engine was in widespread operation.

From the outset these engines polarised into very definite forms; they were either side or saddle tanks, and either four or six coupled. The 0–4–0s had the ability to negotiate the tightest of curves, and to go virtually wherever a wagon could. Accordingly, these engines found favour in docks, ironworks, quarries, power stations and factories, whereas the 0–6–0 came to prevalence in collieries and the larger mines.

During its evolution on the standard gauge the 0–4–0's cylinder sizes progressed from 7 in. in diameter to 15 in., whilst the 0–6–0 ranged from 11 in. to 18 in. Driving wheel diameters

The crane tank was a fascinating variation on the conventional industrial and first appeared in 1866. This delightful engine is one of a handful of survivors and her duty is to carry tree trunks up to the sawmill at a railway sleeper factory in Northern India. She was built to the order of the Secretary of State for India in 1903 by Manning Wardle of Leeds, although her crane structures and auxiliary engines came from the nearby works of Joseph Booth and Brothers of Rodley. Before the engine arrived, the work was performed by elephants.

117

were a mean 3 ft. on the 0–4–0 and 4 ft. on the 0–6–0, and whereas the smallest 0–4–0 weighed as little as 12 tons in full working order, the largest of the 0–6–0s topped 50 tons.

Many such engines were built to gauges smaller than standard and their dimensions were reduced accordingly. Thousands of industrials have worked in Britain in addition to a vast export market which distributed identical or similar engines all over the world.

The last steam locomotives to work in Britain were industrials and although in recent years most were of standard gauge, many of the earlier examples were built to smaller gauges. As has been mentioned, most industrials were small by comparison with main-line engines but some interesting exceptions have occurred, especially in South Africa where the hauls from the pitheads to the main line are often lengthy and heavily graded. In such instances, powerful engines – often of main-line proportions – are used, including Garratts and some specially built 4–8–2T/ 4–8–4Ts from North British.

However the greater percentage of exported industrials were built to gauges narrower than standard, particularly those intended for plantation work where tracks were cheaply and hastily built and possibly slewed from one operational area to another. These gauges centred around 2 ft. 0 in., 2 ft. 6 in., 3 ft. 0 in., one metre and 3 ft. 6 in., with variations in between.

Often engines for the narrower gauges demanded an extra carrying wheel which gave rise to the 0–4–2T. Side tanks, saddle tanks, pannier tanks and well tanks were all featured and in some cases tenders were provided if the locomotive was to burn such waste items as bagasse (sugar cane waste). This provided a category of engine not generally encountered in Britain, known as the tender-tank type.

Britain's industrials were superbly built and many survive all over the world. Most of the private British locomotive builders exported industrials but Leeds was undeniably the centre of production, having four celebrated foundries in one small parish: Manning Wardle, Kitsons, Hudswell Clarke and Hunslet.

Just north of the Scottish border the town of Kilmarnock established a prolific locomotive building industry in which Andrew Barclay were to become world renowned and their standard gauge designs were of an unmistakable family lineage. The neighbouring works of Dick Kerr also built for various industries around the world.

Other great centres were Stafford, where the wonderful products from Bagnall's Castle engine works were built, Bristol (Pecket and Avonside), Stoke-on-Trent (Kerr Stuart) and Newcastle (Hawthorn Leslie).

In contrast, the major builders in the private sector, Beyer Peacock, Robert Stephenson, Vulcan Foundry and North British, concentrated primarily upon the production of engines for main-line service.

Suburban tanks

The expansion of cities under industrial revolution created a pattern of urban living which was becoming widely established by the middle of the nineteenth century. The subsequent need for frequent and rapid communications gave birth to the suburban steam train. This aspect of railway operation hastened a change in the entire pattern of British society by providing easy and rapid travel from home to place of work, and thus enabling commerce to become centralised within the cities.

In Britain, the true suburban tank evolved during the 1860s with Beyer Peacock's handsome 4–4–0Ts. Thenceforth, as the need for this type of engine increased, a delightful variety of wheel arrangements were adopted by the various railway companies especially for services around London but for similar work in other leading cities as well. Especially prevalent were 0–4–4Ts, 2–4–2Ts, 0–6–2Ts, 4–4–2Ts, 4–6–2Ts, 4–6–4Ts, and in the later years 2–6–2Ts and 2–6–4Ts.

It will be seen that throughout its evolution the suburban tank engine progressed in size and power. Trains grew heavier as cities and suburbs expanded, whilst coaching stock steadily increased in weight. Moreover, the public's demand for faster timings on commuter trains exerted further pressure both on locomotive design and methods of operation.

Sadly, few true suburbans exist in the world today owing to their services being a natural target for electrification or in some cases 'dieselisation'. In Britain conversion from steam began as long ago as the early 1920s with the widespread electrification of the Southern network. Many countries to which Britain supplied locomotives had limited need for suburban services as such – the greatest users being the European nations and North America who, in general, were responsible for building their own suburban locomotives.

One of the most dynamic British-built suburban services were those around the Argentinian capital Buenos Aires. For half a century these were brilliantly performed by three-cylinder 2–6–4Ts assisted by the 8A class 2–6–2 which were built in Glasgow during the Edwardian period. Sadly the three-cylinder engines are but a memory although a number of 8As still exist on secondary duties. For its busy services around Montevideo, neighbouring Uruguay used the very attractive 4–4–4Ts described in Chapter 2.

In India, steam has been replaced on most of the densely worked suburban services but examples of the handsome WM class 2–6–4Ts built by the Vulcan foundry and Robert Stephenson and Hawthorn between 1939 and 1964 remain at work. A larger version also survives in the form of the WT class 2–8–4Ts which, although built at Chittaranjan, are very British in aspect.

The finest suburban workings left in India are the busy services radiating from Secunderabad. These are worked by the sprightly YM class 2–6–4Ts which, despite being built by Nippon in 1956, are very similar in appearance to the WMs. Even here the prowess of the YMs is under constant challenge from the 'middle class' commuters who, ever aspirant, demand that the South Central Railway authorities electrify the system.

Branch tanks

Britain's home railways had a tradition of down grading suburban engines to branch-line work. Many of the country's branch lines were not built until the end of the nineteenth century by which time displaced suburbans were available and if such engines were small and rather worn out the pace on many rural branches was infinitely less demanding than the intense activities around cities. Thus a close correlation exists between suburban and branch types and many common designs were prepared using four-coupled tanks up to the turn of the century and six-coupled arrangements thenceforth.

A marked contrast occurred between Britain's home practice and the circumstances which prevailed in many of the countries to which Britain exported. The majority of developing nations had few branch lines as we know them. The main lines themselves were in their *modus operandi* rather like branches and where lines that were clearly secondary did exist, they were invariably very long and thus required fully fledged main-line engines to work them, albeit with lighter axle loads than normal.

The great exception to this rule is the Indian subcontinent which has the most fascinating variety of branch and cross-country lines imaginable. Three principal gauges are represented: 2 ft. 0 in., 2 ft. 6 in. and one metre. These lines employ a marvellous diversity of motive power which in most cases was specially designed for branch service. India's narrow gauge branches are the closest one can find to the traditional English branch; the motive power, method of operation and atmosphere are all unmistakeable. The heavily populated rural areas of India render the branch/cross-country lines a vital aspect of regional communication exactly as they once did in Britain. On some of these networks, the arrival of a train is an event to be savoured and not hurried.

Other examples exist, not least in Java, but throughout large parts of the world the appalling rate at which road transport has developed has caused many branch/secondary lines to be abandoned.

Shunting tanks

The shunting engine as we know it did not appear until the mid nineteenth century. It took 30 years for Britain's main-line railway network to become sufficiently coordinated to merit locomotives being specially designed for shunting. During the interim period main-line engines undertook whatever yard movements were necessary but once the national network took shape the formation of trains at important junctions became ever more complex and goods yards became an integral part of the system.

The standard British shunting engine was an 0-6-0 tank of either side, saddle or pannier variety. Such engines were easily moved in either direction and valuable adhesion for heavy shunting was gained by the weight of the fuel bearing directly onto the driving wheels.

The golden years of the British shunter were between 1875 and 1930, for afterwards the diesel began to make its presence felt on such duties whilst simultaneously numerous older types from the late Victorian period – particularly the inside-cylinder 0-6-0 – were being displaced on main-line duty and gravitated into the marshalling yards to eke out their days. Both of these events stunted the shunting tank's development. It is an interesting reflection that throughout its entire evolutionary period the basic British shunter remained remarkably similar, expanding but slightly over successive decades.

The vast majority of countries to which Britain supplied locomotives had little need for droves of specially designed shunting engines. Their railway networks were by British standards extremely sparse and in many instances stations or junctions which received only a limited number of freights per day were adequately shunted by the train engines and only at certain strategically important junctions was any type of shunting engine necessary. Therefore – as in the case of other types of engine previously discussed – the shunting tank proper was essentially a product of the industrialised nations to whom Britain's locomotive exports were limited and the definitive shunting tank as we know it in Britain was never prolific in the world at large.

Even on a vast network like South Africa's, shunting has – in general – been performed by downgraded main-liners and much the same applied in Rhodesia, Mozambique and Angola. In contrast, Nigeria and Sudan both have shunting tanks; 0–8–0Ts in the former and 0–6–0Ts – of typical British Great Eastern appearance – in the latter.

One would expect the densely operated 5 ft. 6 in.-gauge network of India to have standard shunting designs but for many years down-graded inside-cylinder 0–6–0s seem to have sufficed, whilst today displaced WG 2–8–2s are to be seen fulfilling the role. Burma Railways, however, does have several classic 0–6–0Ts and 0–6–0STs.

In Latin America, the enclaves of almost exclusively British motive power in Uruguay, Paraguay and parts of Brazil exclude a true shunting engine, although Paraguay did have some Hawthorn Leslie 0–6–0Ts but these have long since disappeared. Argentina, whose railways are denser than those of other Latin American countries, has employed several classes of 0–6–0STs both on the standard and 5 ft. 6 in.-gauge and the example illustrated is in the very finest of British home traditions.

Some interesting subdivisions of shunting engine appeared and included the crane tank, Sentinel and humper. The crane engine was usually a conventional tank with a crane attached. Considerable numbers were built and the type was invariably used for specialised service in particular yards.

The Sentinel on the other hand was a half-way stage between the steam locomotive and the diesel. Built by Sentinel of Shrewsbury, these vertical-boilered engines with chain drive were incredibly powerful for their size and the makers claimed they were the most significant advance ever made on the conventional shunting engine.

Equally fascinating was the humper which appeared in small numbers in Britain and other parts of the world. These engines were designed for large marshalling yards which adopted the hump system in which wagons were pushed uncoupled up an incline and allowed to roll by gravity into whichever siding was appropriate. Such yards obviously demanded bigger locomotives than the traditional 0–6–0 and this genre of engines began dramatically in 1907 when Robinson produced a three-cylinder 0–8–4T for the Great Central Railway. The last British humpers on earth disappeared as recently as 1976 when two massive 2–10–2Ts which had been built by Nasmyth Wilson were tragically broken up in Bombay.

The last remnants of the British shunting tradition have become rare beasts today, their diminishing ranks being constantly challenged either by dieselisation or the ever increasing numbers of newer and more powerful main-liners made redundant by modernisation.

A magnificent heavy duty side tank built to a standard design by Hawthorn Leslie storms across an old slag bank at Kulti Iron Works in Bengal. Built in 1927, this engine is similar to the type later adopted in Britain for heavy hauling at power stations.

Left: This delightful 0–4–0ST is one of the last industrial locomotives to remain in British service. She works at the Castle Donington power station in the English midlands and was built by Robert Stephenson and Hawthorn of Newcaslte in 1955. Although she is a comparatively modern engine, her basic design was conceived by Hawthorn Leslie during the early years of the century.

Overleaf: The Sentinel is a rare beast today and I was thrilled to discover this one active at a wagon works in Brazil. Built by Sentinel of Shrewsbury these engines had vertical high-pressure boilers and chain drive. Sentinel claimed their engines to be infinitely cheaper to run than the conventional industrial and some 850 were built for service all over the world between 1923 and 1957.

Left: A Hunslet Austerity 0–6–0ST prepares to draw a rake of freshly lifted coals away from the Eccles Washery on the Backworth system north of the Tyne. The Hunslet Austerity is the best known British industrial type and following its introduction for wartime service in 1943, it spread to Britain's coalfields and building continued until 1964. The Austerities are almost certainly the most numerous preserved class in the world with over 60 examples saved.

Overleaf: It was not often that the 0–6–0 industrial was increased in size but it did progress to an 0–6–2T for the Calcutta Port Trust who have employed these chunky side tanks for some 40 years. The type was first introduced by Hunslet of Leeds in 1945 although some later batches came from Henschel of Germany and Mitsubishi Heavy Industries of Japan. Building continued until 1955 and the class finally totalled 45 engines.

Left: Here is an industrial tank of very advanced design. She is a 4–8–2T specially built for goldfield service in South Africa by North British of Glasgow in 1940. She is caught heading a rake of freshly won gold ore from the mine to the reduction plant where the gold is sifted.

Overleaf: If any evidence were needed that Indian Railways mirrored those of the mother country this magnificent 0–6–4T would supply it. She was built by the Vulcan Foundry in 1915 for the East Indian Railway as their CT class. Following withdrawal from main-line service she was sold in 1967 to Rohtas Industries where she survives today.

This rare engine epitomises the suburban tank engine of her day, the 0–6–4T representing a mid-period phase in the evolution of suburban steam traction.

Argentina's 8A class 2–6–2Ts were exported from the Clyde in 1906/7. The class totalled 34 engines and all came from North British. Their principal duty was to operate the intense suburban services around Buenos Aires. After displacement from this work many gravitated onto branch lines or shunting duties. The survivors are now 75 years old and they still retain their original boilers.

Above: A typical Indian branch-line scene on the delightful 2 ft.-6 in.-gauge line from Burdwan to Katwa in Bengal. The engine is No. 3, an 0–6–4T built by Bagnall of Stafford in 1914. This lovely line was originally worked by McLeod and Co. but has been under Eastern Railway ownership since 1966.

Right: The last word in Indian suburban tanks are these magnificent WT class 2–8–4Ts, 30 of which were built by the Chittaranjan Locomotive Works between 1959/67. They are capable of lifting heavy trains, have a rapid acceleration rate and are impressive engines in every respect. This engine, No. 14011 was built in 1965 and is based at Rajamundry for working cross-country passenger trains around the Godavri Delta in Andhra Pradesh.

138

Left: Another extremely rare engine is this classic main-line shunting tank seen hard at work on the 5 ft.-6 in.-gauge at Bahia Blanca in Argentina. She belongs to the BE class first introduced by North British in 1904 and subsequently built by Kerr Stuart of Stoke-on-Trent. These engines have a delightful Scottish aura and appear to be a larger version of the Caledonian Railway's famous Pug 0–4–0ST. The BEs were, in effect, a standard shunting tank for the 5 ft.-6 in.-gauge railways of Argentina. The engine illustrated – No. 2562 – came from Kerr Stuart in 1913 and is possibly the last example left in service today.

Overleaf: This scene on the 2 ft.-6 in.-gauge Dehri Rohtas Light Railway depicts KC class No. 26 built by North British in 1905 at the head of a train of limestone bound for the Rohtas cement factory at Dehri-on-Sone. Originally this engine worked on the famous Kalka-Simla Railway prior to being sold to Rohtas Industries along with four sister engines in 1967.

Index